when GOOD THINGS happen to BAD PEOPLE

when GOOD THINGS happen to BAD PEOPLE

PATRICIA KLATCH SHENYO

FAITH GREATER THAN THE MUSTARD SEED

When Good Things Happen To Bad People

Copyright © 2023 by Patricia Klatch Shenyo
and Christopher A. Shenyo

PKS Books

Printed in the United States of America

All rights reserved. No part of this book may be used
or reproduced in any manner whatsoever
without written permission from the author.

ISBN: 979-8-89109-585-4 - paperback
ISBN: 979-8-89109-586-1 - ebook

All Biblical references are taken from:

Saint Joseph Holy Bible, Douay Version,
Catholic Book Publishing Company, New York

The New American Bible, Thomas Nelson Publishers,
Nashville, Camden, New York.

Dedication

This book is dedicated to
Each and every human person
In the entire world –
Whoever was, is now, and
Whoever shall be –
The born and the unborn
Because of the inestimable
Worth and dignity of
Each human person
Made in the image and likeness of
God Who is Father, Son, and Holy Spirit.

Table of Contents

Introduction: What Does It Mean? ix

I - What and Who is GOD?

Chapter 1 - What And Who Is God ?. 1
Chapter 2 - Does God Really Exist? 7
Chapter 3 - Is God All Merciful? 13
Chapter 4 - What Does God Want? 21

II - The Good, the Bad, the Ugly, and the Irredeemable? 33

Chapter 1 - The Good: Who Are They? 35
Chapter 2 - The Bad: How Bad Are We? 53
Chapter 3 - The Ugly: Can They Be Saved? 75
Chapter 4 - The Irredeemable – Is Anyone Irredeemable?. 99

III - Why Suffering? & Why Forgiveness? 115

Chapter 1 - Why Does God Allow Suffering?. 117
Chapter 2 - Oh God, Why ME?. 125
Chapter 3 - Why Forgiveness? 135
Chapter 4 - Why Should I Forgive? .141

IV - Prayers –Do They Work? Does God Listen To Me? 155

Chapter 1 - God, Can You Hear Me?....................157
Chapter 2 - Some Misconceptions? 167

V - Miracles! Miracles – Really? 179

Chapter 1 - Do You Believe In Miracles? 181
Chapter 2 - Do Miracles Still Happen?....................187
Chapter 3 - What are Eucharistic Miracles? 195

VI -Where Are We? Are We Done?

Chapter 1 - Do We Know God Better Now? 207
Chapter 2 - Where Do We Go From Here? 213

VII - Conclusion – What's in it for You and for Me?... 219

Conclusion - What Can We Expect? 221
Appendix A - The Ten Commandments...................229
Appendix B - Mary Mother Of God......................237
Appendix C - The Abortion Issue........................241
Appendix D - The Warning: Illumination Of Conscience And The Miracle...247
Bibiography 251
Order Information..................................255
About the Author...................................257

Introduction
What Does It Mean?

When good things happen to bad people seems to be a rather strange topic for a book. How did this come about?

I happened to acquire an old 1985 VHS video entitled, "When Bad Things Happen to Good People" in which Rabbi Harold S. Kushner explains how he came to write his book with the same title. Amazon.com is a great place to acquire almost anything, so I sent for the book.

Rabbi Kushner describes how through his own personal pain he came to know, understand, and appreciate the enigmatic presence of a loving and compassionate God who doesn't just sit and watch painful human drama, but suffers along with us. God suffers? How can that be?

Before we can answer those questions, we need to know something about God. Who and what is God? What is God like? Does God really exist? How do we know? If there is a God, does He really care? Does He care about *ME*? How can I know that?

OK, so maybe God does care about me. But does He care about everyone else, too? There are all kinds of people. I'm sure that He cares about the good and caring people, the loving people who go out of their way to do good, to help others in need. What about those who are not so caring, those who only worry about themselves? Does God love them a little less? How about those who are difficult to get along with, those who have a tendency to use others to promote their own agenda, not caring if someone else gets hurt along the way? We all know some of them, don't we? Is God more distant from them?

Then there are those people who cause problems for themselves and for others by deliberately breaking the law. They usually get caught and end up incarcerated. People tend to stay away from them. Does God also stay away?

If you watch the news or read the newspapers, you must be aware of the really evil people who murder innocent people, the dictators who murder thousands of their own people, the human traffickers who kidnap people and force them into some type of slavery. How could anyone love such horrible people? How could God love or care about them? Does God care?

WOW! Those are a lot of thought provoking questions. Do we know the answers? Let's find out. Come along with me as we search together.

One suggestion I would like to make to you – read this book from beginning to end. Don't skip around as some people like to do. The reason is that it builds on itself as you read along, and you will achieve a more complete understanding of its profound and sublime message. Skipping around will defeat that purpose.

Note: All the stories in this book are true. Some of the names have been changed for privacy purposes.

I
What and Who is GOD?

CHAPTER 1

What And Who Is God?

Are we going to question God?

Is it appropriate to question the Almighty? How can we, finite beings that we are, be so presumptuous as to have the audacity to question the Infinite? How will God view this bare-faced boldness? Is this in anyway threatening or insulting to God? Let's get real. God is bigger than that. That's right. If a person comes before Him with humility and a sincere heart desiring to know God better, I believe that this would be very pleasing to God, for to know God is to love Him. I believe that God would welcome any and all inquiries designed to have a more complete understanding of Himself and would lead him/her to a clearer realization of the answers being sought. Such a person would be drawn into a closer relationship with God. Isn't that what is desired?

But what about a person who is filled with arrogance and pride, who perhaps wants to disprove the existence of God, or maybe that God is so far above us that He does not really care. Will God ignore such questions or attempts to contradict or question His goodness? Will He be angry, viewing this as disrespect, irreverence, or blasphemous? Will God be vengeful toward such a person, punish him/her?

Again, God is bigger than that. Remember, no one can hurt God. God will allow and, I believe, welcome this person to pursue his doubts and gently but firmly lead him/her to the truth.

If you are an agnostic, atheist, or an incredulous type, stay with me. As we go on, we will uncover some amazing things. Whether or not you choose to believe them is up to you.

Robert W. Faid is such a person. As a nuclear scientist he believed that the Bible and science contradicted each other and that science was right. Imagine that – science knowing more than God! Unbelievable! After facing death with terminal cancer, being prayed for by Christians, and making a miraculous recovery, (more about miracles later) he decided to put his scientific knowledge to work and began to search the so-called "myths" in the Bible. Read for yourself the fascinating and astounding results of his investigations. They can be found in his book, *A Scientific Approach To Biblical Mysteries*, a 2 in 1 book that you can get from Guideposts, Carmel, NY 10512, or go to their website at www.guideposts.org. You can also check on the Internet, Amazon.com, or at bookstores.

Can God be defined?

God is an intelligence of the highest caliber, the extent of which it is impossible to comprehend. God is a power unparalleled by any other, a force against which none can stand. God is an uncreated being, simple in essence, and at the same time the Supreme Being highest above all else. According to St. Thomas Aquinas, God is absolutely simple; that is, God is not composed of parts, or compounded elements, not material. God is perfection without flaws of any kind. WOW! This is the kind of stuff that just blows one's mind! The most learned of theologians have difficulty explaining God. Since my knowledge is so limited, I am keeping this as simple as possible, not only for your sake, but for mine as well.

Let's look at some of the attributes of God:

God is the Supreme Good. All that He does is good. The Bible tells us, "God looked at everything He had made, and He found it very good." (Genesis 1:31)

God is omnipresent. He is present to and in all things. He always remains the same, never changing. He is eternal – without a beginning, without an end. Now that is heavy. I can understand something without an end that goes on forever. I do have a problem with something that has no beginning. To me this is mind boggling, beyond what my human mind is capable of fathoming, a complete mystery that I can only take on faith. Does it boggle your mind, also?

God knows all things all at the same time and in every detail. He knows everything about you, about me, about everyone that has ever lived and will ever be. He knows our most secret thoughts and desires even before we know them ourselves. He knows the past, the present, and yes, He even knows the future. God is truth. God can neither deceive nor be deceived.

God is love. He loves everything and everyone that He has created. He loves you and He loves me in spite of our faults and shortcomings, in spite of our sins.

God is mercy and at the same time justice. We deserve to reap the consequences of our actions. When we do wrong, we must answer for it. We can't make excuses, not to ourselves and not to God. Sometimes we lie to ourselves or try to rationalize our behavior, but we can't lie to God. Remember God *knows* all things. We can, however, seek forgiveness from God Who always responds with mercy to the repentant heart. He welcomes a sinner back with open arms and with joy. Check out the parable of the Prodigal Son (Luke 15:11-32) for a more in-depth verification of God's greatest attribute, that of His unfathomable mercy.

Is God male or female?

God is spirit having no material body, and therefore, has no gender. You may have noticed that I have been referring to God as "He." In the Bible God said, "Let Us make man in Our image." (Genesis 1:26) God is One. "Us" and "Our" denotes more than one. In the New Testament of the Bible we are told by Jesus that God, being One, consists of the Father, Jesus the Son, and the Holy Spirit. While God is One, there are three distinct persons in God. Hard to understand? – a mystery! Jesus refers to God as Father, a male figure. Jesus, Himself is male. If He is one and the same with the Father, "The Father and I are one." (John 11:30), it only stands to reason that God is referred to as male. This would include the Holy Spirit as all three are one God. A bit confusing? Welcome to the club. In more recent times some have tried to portray God as a woman. Ridiculous! Jesus calls God "Abba" (Father) and father is male. Jesus would know, after all He is God's Son. Why is it that some people try to make God into their own perceived images?

Is God a racist?

Let's think about this. In our United States of America in more recent years, we have been hearing about white supremacy and oppression of minority peoples such as the Blacks, Hispanics, Asians, and Native American Indians. While it is true that in generations past these people were treated badly, in no other country on this planet are there more opportunities for them to achieve their dreams. I believe that God especially formed and allowed the United States to grow into a great and wonderful place for all peoples to come together and live in dignity and liberty. As a young country, less than 300 years old, dedicated to God by George Washington himself, we have become the most prosperous and welcoming nation than any other in the world.

Some radical groups have been trying to divide the American people by claiming that we are oppressive and racist. Black Lives Matter and Antifa groups have been trying to destroy our country by tearing down statues, monuments, and removing historical names such as Washington, Jefferson, and other historical figures from schools and governmental buildings because they were slave owners. They even wanted to destroy Abraham Lincoln who was responsible for freeing the slaves at the cost of many lives during the Civil War. Some are even trying to rewrite history books wanting to teach our children an untrue and alternate founding of our nation. Does this make any sense to you?

Also, consider this – if the Black slaves were never brought to our country, where would their descendants be today in Africa? What kind of life would they have? Would they even exist? Here in our country many descendants of slaves, now free, are educated, and have achieved remarkable success and status.

How does God view all this?

God is a Being of love and truth. Rewriting history does not change what took place. We are all imperfect human beings. We make decisions and mistakes – some with good intentions, some with selfish motives. However, you cannot change what took place many years ago. We can only strive to correct our mistakes and improve our circumstances for the benefit of our people. But do we do that? God wants us to learn to love each other. That is the reason our country came to be with so many different peoples and cultures.

Did you ever watch the 1991 movie, *Robin Hood: Prince of Thieves* starring Kevin Costner and Morgan Freeman? There is a particular scene in which Robin Hood (Kevin Costner) having returned home to England brought with him a black-skinned Moore (Morgan Freemen) who is the only non-white person in the camp. A little girl comes up to him and says, "Did God paint you?" He replies, "Did God paint me? For certain." The girl asks, "Why?" And the answer comes, "Because Allah (God) loves wondrous variety."

What do you think about this? God has created infinite variety. No two snowflakes are exactly alike. Look at all the countless leaves on the trees. No two are exactly alike. What about all the varieties, colors, shapes of the flowers, animals, birds, sea creatures, etc. No two are exactly alike. God loves all of His creations.

What about human beings? Again, God created an infinite variety of people – different skin colors, eyes, hair textures, sizes, shapes, talents, intelligence, abilities, and even disabilities. No two are exactly alike, not even identical twins. There is only one trait that we all have in common – we are all created in the image and likeness of God. Why did God create us this way? God is love. He loves all His children. He wants us to learn to love each other and to accept each other regardless of our differences and circumstances. What a wonderful and happy world this would be if more people took this to heart and treated each other with respect and dignity. Don't you think so? That is the reason that God is very much grieved when any of His children are purposely destroyed through war, murder, torture, abortion – because of greed, false pride, or selfishness.

How great, wondrous, and awesome is our God!

Chapter 2

Does God Really Exist?

Can we really prove that there is a God?

An astounding YES! How? It's simple really. Take a look around you for a moment. Look at the trees, the flowers, and the mountains – such incredible beauty. Jesus said of the wildflowers, "Yet I assure you Solomon in all his splendor was not arrayed like one of these." (Matthew 6:29)

There was a beautiful daffodil plant that grew by our house on the side of the chimney. Every spring it came up bearing lovely yellow flowers that danced in the breeze. Then one summer my husband decided to have an asphalt walkway installed leading from the front of the house to the back. The daffodil plant was completely covered over with thick black asphalt. That was the end of this delicate flower that smiled in the sun, or so we thought. The following spring, to our utter amazement, that daffodil pushed its way up through the asphalt forming sort of a flowerpot out of the asphalt. Every spring it is the first plant to come up, warmed no doubt by the sun shining on the black asphalt. This is a delicate flower which I could easily tear apart with my fingers yet it has the strength to push itself up through thick asphalt without so much as a tear in its leaves or fragile petals. I know that I for one would not be able to push my fingers through that thick asphalt without getting them all bloody. Could you? I call this my flower that has faith "greater than the mustard seed." Who could create a living thing so beautiful so delicate yet so strong – only God!

Planet Earth is incredibly beautiful even though some areas have been exploited and destroyed by mankind. There are innumerable species of plants, birds, animals, fish and creatures of the oceans and seas. Each is a living creation and is programmed to know exactly what is required of it in order to survive and perpetuate itself. Who is the Programmer? Someone had to design and give life to all of these.

Did you ever see a tiny red spider? It is bright red and smaller than the head of a stickpin. Yet this tiny creature knows how to feed and care for itself, travel where it wishes to go, reproduce itself, and whatever else it does. What kind of super intelligence could have designed such a miniature marvel? Not even the greatest scientific mind that ever lived could accomplish that.

Yes, with all our modern technology, engineering, and imagination we can create wonderful products such as robots that can respond to spoken commands. We have already put a man on the moon. With incredible accuracy we have the ability to shoot and destroy missiles that could harm us out of the sky. Fantastic? You bet! And these are just a few of incredible accomplishments of modern science and ingenuity, not to mention those we haven't even heard about yet. But, and this is a big one, they cannot create a *living* entity from nothing or even from an inanimate substance. Why is that? Simple – they are not God.

What else is there?

Look up at the night sky – all those stars. Astronomers have discovered through the use of giant telescopes planets, constellations, black holes, and who knows what else is out there in that immense space. In our own solar system the planets orbit around the sun in an orderly fashion. Who could have created such vastness all orchestrated in perfect harmony? Could it have come about all by itself? Impossible! The only plausible answer – you guessed it, God.

Let's take one last example. Get a mirror and look at yourself. What do you see? What color are your eyes? How tall are you? Is your hair curly, wavy, or straight? Is your heart pumping without you constantly being conscious of it? Can you talk, walk, dance, use your hands to do things? Can you think, plan, decide, and be creative? Can you express your emotions and communicate your thoughts to another person? How is all this possible? Someone had to design you, program you, and breathe life into you for you to even exist. How can anyone conceive of the idea that there is no God? Incredible!

Some years ago someone came out with the theory that God is dead. That's pure stupidity. If God could die, then He couldn't be God, could He? That's common sense pure and simple. Some people lack common sense. Nothing more needs to be said.

How can we ask God?

Still have a few little doubts rambling around in your brain? Let's check out something else. Let's ask God Himself. How can we do this and expect Him to answer us? What about the Bible? It's supposed to be the Word of God. Can we trust the Bible? After all it was written by Moses and other human beings. Or was it? Some believe that the Bible was written merely by persons who dealt mostly with the history of the Jewish people. Others believe that, while this is true, the Bible is the inspired Word of God. What is the truth?

The Bible's claim to Divine Inspiration is "All scripture is given by inspiration of God, and is profitable for doctrine, for reproof, for correction, for instruction in righteousness." (2 Timothy 3:16) This tells us that God *overshadowed* the minds and hearts of the writers of the Bible, that is, the original manuscripts of the Old Testament that were written in Hebrew as well as the New Testament written in Greek.

According to the Catechism of the Catholic Church, the author of the Sacred Scripture is God Himself. The following excerpts are taken from the Catechism of the Catholic Church:

> "The divinely revealed realities, which are contained and presented in the text of Sacred Scripture, have been written down under the inspiration of the Holy Spirit. . .they have God as their author and have been handed on as such to the Church herself."

Weren't the books of the Bible written by humans?

The human authors of the various books of the Bible were inspired by God.

> "To compose the sacred books, God chose certain men who, all the while He employed them in this task, made full use of their own faculties and powers so that, though He acted in them, it was as true authors that they consigned to writing whatever He wanted written, and no more."

How do we know that the Bible teaches the truth?

The inspired books of the Bible teach the truth because God is truth Who cannot deceive nor be deceived.

"Since therefore all that the inspired authors or sacred writers affirm should be regarded as affirmed by the Holy Spirit, we must acknowledge that the books of Scripture firmly, faithfully, and without error teach that truth which God, for the sake of our salvation, wished to see confided to the Sacred Scriptures."[1]

It has been determined that the Bible is accurate archeologically, historically, and scientifically. No human person could have created this. Dr. David Kazhdan, Chairman, Mathematics Department, Harvard University states, "This is real research by real researchers. No human could have done this let alone that it is prophetic."

The Old Testament reveals God's plan for our salvation. It explains the Covenant with the Jewish people and the promise of the Messiah or Redeemer. This promise was fulfilled in Jesus Christ Who came not to abolish the law but to fulfill it. Jesus came to better reveal the Father's love and mercy toward us. Jesus came to pay the price for our sins through His passion, death, and resurrection so that we may have eternal life. All this is foretold in the Old Testament and accomplished in the New Testament.

You are not sure about this? Read the Scriptures. Study them and find out for yourself the correlation and accuracy of the prophesies regarding the coming of the Messiah. If you are having difficulty with understanding something in the Bible, join a Bible study group. Choose a group that is led by a member of the clergy or someone who has formally studied the Sacred Scriptures. Don't be afraid to ask questions.

---

1 *Catechism of the Catholic Church*, Libreria Editrice Vaticana, English Translation for the United States of America, 1994 United States Catholic Conference, Inc., p. 31

Is God in control of everything?

We know that God created all things. He knows all things. He commands the winds and the rain, the forces of nature, the movement of the planets. Is He in complete control of everything? Is there anything that He does not control? Yes, there is something that God does not control and that is our free will. God chose to give us free will, and He will not renege on that.

Since God respects our free will, does He give up on you if you do not want to follow Him, if you do not keep His commandments? God does not give up on anyone. God loves each and every one of us, and He pursues us giving each one of us the graces we need to find Him. We don't even have to ask Him. He knows how to get to us. God is very patient. He waits for a little glimmer from us of hope, of curiosity, of sorrow, of wanting to know the truth. He is constantly ready with His grace and His help for us. We can accept or reject His grace. He has given us free will.

At this point you may be tempted to ask, "What about *me*? Why doesn't God pursue *me*? Doesn't He love *me*? Does He really care about **ME**? Oh, but He does. He gently leads us but never forces us to accept Him or His graces. You might say, "I don't see any evidence of Him pursuing *me*." Oh, no? You are reading this book, aren't you?

Stay with me and find out how much more there is to learn about the love and goodness of God and how He leads *you* to Himself and to ETERNAL LIFE!

Chapter 3

Is God All Merciful?

Who is the Holy Trinity?

The Holy Trinity, though One God, is comprised of three *distinct* persons – the Father, Jesus the Son, and the Holy Spirit. How do we know this? In the Old Testament of the Bible we read, "Then God said, 'Let **Us** make man in **Our** image...'(Genesis 1:26) "Us" and "Our" denote more than one person. Each person is distinct from the others, yet they are all one. How can that be? Is each of these three persons a part of God? No, they are all in each other and yet are distinct from each other. Hard to understand? Without a doubt. We as finite beings cannot fully understand this mystery.

The brilliant mind of St. Thomas Aquinas gives us a rather simple clue. "Distinction does not necessarily mean separation...the whiteness and coldness of snow are really distinct from each other, and each is really distinct from the substance of snow, although there is no separating these things."[2] We speak of the Father, the Son, and the Holy Spirit as God, not as Gods. God is One. When God created the

---

2 *A Tour of the Summa.* Msgr. Paul J. Glenn, p. 29

Universe, the Father, the Son, and the Holy Spirit were all involved even though we consider the Father to be the Creator.

Who is God the Father?

Would you like to know God the Father on a more personal level? He would really like that. How do we know? Jesus calls God "Abba" (Father) which is our equivalent of "Daddy." Jesus tells us to call God "Abba" as well. Do you think that God would like us to call Him "Daddy?" He really does want us to be that close to Him so He probably would like it very much if we called Him "Daddy." What a wonderful image of God!

In 1932, Mother Eugenia Elisabetta Ravasio (1907-1990) received a visit from God the Father. (Yes, God can do that.) Here is the real purpose of His coming and some of the highlights of His message:

> To banish the excessive fear that My Creatures have of Me as the Just Judge and to show them that My joy lies in being known and loved by My Children.
>
> To bring hope to men and nations so they will live in peace and security working for their salvation.
>
> In the Old Testament I created prophets and told them My desires, My sorrows, My joys so that the prophets could communicate them to everyone. The more evil grew. . .I was obliged to be strict in order to reprove them – not to punish them. . .but to lead them back to their Creator. When evil overwhelmed men's hearts, I was compelled to send calamities upon the earth to purify men through suffering, the destruction of their possessions, and even death.
>
> I promised the world a Messiah Who is God Whom I sent in Jesus, My Son. Yet We are One. Therefore, in My Son, they

would crucify Me to bring about my death. But My love for My children was too great to stop. Understand well that I loved you more than My beloved Son, or rather, more than Myself. Love was the guiding principle in it all. Even if your sins were as repulsive as mud, your confidence and your love will make Me forget them, so you will not be judged. I am just, it is true, but love pays for everything. . .you will be judged with infinitely merciful love.[3]

God, our Father, is infinitely good, infinitely rich, and infinitely merciful. He will give us everything we need if we ask Him. He desires that we share everything with Him, our joys, our sorrows, our needs, our sufferings, and our desires. He wants to take care of us in this life so that we can avoid evil. He has great plans for us. *And He wants us to ultimately share the glories of heaven with Him for all eternity.* Where else could we ever find a father like Father God?

Who is Jesus Christ?

Jesus is God, the second person of the Holy Trinity. Why did He come to earth to live among us? Approximately 2000 years ago, He came to earth, born of a woman, the Virgin Mary, conceived by the power of the Holy Spirit. How do we know that this is true?

First, it was prophesized in the Old Testament, "Therefore the Lord Himself will give you this sign: the virgin shall be with child, and bear a son, and shall call His name Immanuel." (Isaiah 7:14)

Second, it is recorded in the Gospels, "Now this is how the birth of Jesus Christ came about. When His mother, Mary, was engaged to Joseph, but before they lived together, she was found with child through the power of the Holy Spirit." (Matthew 1:18) ". . .the Angel Gabriel was sent from God. . .to a virgin betrothed to a man named Joseph, of the house of David. The virgin's name was Mary. . .The

---

3　*The Father Speaks To His Children.* "Pater" Publications, pp. 19-25

angel went on to say to her. . . 'You shall conceive and bear a son and you will give Him the name Jesus. Great will be His dignity and He will be called Son of the Most High'. . .Mary said to the angel, 'How can this be since I do not know man?' The angel answered her, 'The Holy Spirit will come upon you and the power of the Most High will overshadow you; hence the holy offspring to be born will be called Son of God.'" (Luke 1:26-27, 31-32, 34-35) God greatly humbled Himself and came to earth as the baby Jesus – God born incarnate. He grew up among us and at thirty years of age began His public ministry.

How incredible is this? God, the Most High, all powerful, all knowing, all present, Lord of the Universe in the person of Jesus Christ, came to earth to live among us. He humbled Himself and was subject to His earthly parents, Mary and Joseph his foster father, mere humans. Did He have to do this? No. Then why did He do this?

God Who is all love and mercy, in the person of Jesus Christ, came here for three particular reasons:

> Jesus came here to teach us to love God above all else and each other as ourselves. He taught us how to live good loving lives, to be kind, compassionate, and to be merciful and forgiving.

> He came here to suffer and die for our sins that we might have everlasting life. God's justice demands that we answer for and make restitution for our sins. Being the loving God that He is, He took it upon Himself to pay the price for our transgressions so that we may have eternal life. He suffered crucifixion, the humiliating death of a criminal, in excruciating agony and pain to pay the price for our sins. Is there anyone else who would be willing to do that?

> Jesus rose from the dead (you read that right, He rose from the dead) after being crucified and ascended into heaven. (He did that, too.) Then He sent the Holy Spirit to help us.

Jesus wanted to remain here with us until the end of time, so He gave Himself to us in the Holy Eucharist (remember God can do anything) and He sent the Holy Spirit to be with us and guide us in all aspects of our life.

For those of you who are not Christian and would like to know more about this wonderful loving Son of God, Jesus Christ, the Messiah, may I suggest that you obtain the DVD *Jesus of Nazareth*. This is an excellent movie that tells the story of Jesus Christ; then it would be good to round it out by reading the New Testament of the Bible.

Who is the Holy Spirit?

The Holy Spirit is the third person of the Holy Trinity. It was He Who spoke through the prophets in the Old Testament of the Bible. It was He Who overshadowed Mary when she conceived Jesus in her womb. It was He Whom Jesus sent to us. The Holy Spirit guides the Church that Jesus founded while on earth to continue His work to teach us so that we may more easily achieve our goal of everlasting life which Jesus won for us through His passion and death on the cross.

Now you may be wondering, is there anything that the Holy Spirit does for *me* as an individual? Yes, most definitely. The Holy Spirit enlightens you, He gives you all good spiritual gifts, He leads you to know God better, when you ask Him. He directs your thoughts to help you in your work and everyday endeavors. The Holy Spirit heals you in body, soul, mind, and spirit. He helps you in all your needs. The Holy Spirit empowers you and gives you strength in your afflictions, and most of all He helps you to become holy, more pleasing to God.

Do you mean me?

So you see, God the Father, Jesus the Son, and the Holy Spirit – three persons in one God all work together. God helps each of us individually. That's right, little you and little me, tiny specks that we are in this vast Universe, because He loves *each one* of us as though you or I were the only creature that he created. You might be wondering, does God really love *me* that much? You better believe it! Even in spite of my many sins? Absolutely!

Those of you who don't believe that He loves *you* that much consider this: God, in the person of Jesus Christ would have suffered and died the humiliating, excruciating death on the cross for *you* even if you were the only one that needed to be saved. This is what we mean when we say that **God is Love, that God is all Merciful.**

Close your eyes and ponder that for several minutes.

Are you not completely convinced?

Are you a die-hard atheist who doesn't believe there is a God no matter how plausible the arguments may be, or an agnostic who still isn't sure? Well, how about an engaging challenge? Suppose you are right – there is no God. There is no life after death. By believing in God, life after death, and having hope as I do, what will I lose? Nothing. If there is nothing to lose, then the only thing I lose is the time and energy I put into my belief. When I die, then it's over. Right?

On the other hand, let's suppose I am right. Suppose there really is a God and life after death. What will you lose? If you have no hope of a wonderful life after death with a loving God and rejected God all your life, where will you be? Hell, perhaps? Only God knows that, and you will, too, eventually. I would not want to be in your shoes finding that out the hard way. Perhaps you don't believe in Hell either. That does not guarantee that it does not exist. How foolish to reject a loving God Who always has your best interest at heart and the power to do something about it.

If after reading the above challenge, you find yourself ridiculing or scoffing at the idea, angry that someone would dare challenge your beliefs, maybe no one can blame you. If you feel annoyed but not really caring because you don't intend to change your views, that's OK, too. Do you find the whole idea preposterous and not worthy of your concern? How about a suggestion?

Go back and reread this challenge. This time read it slowly and really think about what it means. Consider very carefully the possibility of what you might be forfeiting if there is indeed a God. How will you answer when asked by God, "What have you done with your live?" Your careful pondering and consideration could make all the difference to your immortal soul.

Let me ask you this – what is the most important thing in your life right now? This is a ***temporary concern*** because life on this earth is temporary. We all die at some time. Even if you live to be 100 years old, that is still a very short time. Think about it.

Now let me ask you – what is the most important aspect of your existence? ***This is an eternal concern.*** Your relationship with or without God will last forever.

Chapter 4

What Does God Want?

How do we know God's will?

God is simplicity. Everything about God is simple. God makes it easy for us. He *tells* us what is expected of us. God gave us the Ten Commandments. What are they?

I, the Lord, am your God, Who brought you out of the land of Egypt, that place of slavery. You shall have no other gods besides Me.

You shall not take the name of the Lord, your God in vain.

Remember to keep holy the Sabbath day.

Honor your father and your mother.

You shall not kill.

You shall not commit adultery.

You shall not steal.

You shall not bear false witness against your neighbor.

You shall not covet your neighbor's wife.

You shall not covet your neighbor's goods.

(Exodus 20:1-17)
(See Appendix A –
The Ten Commandments for an explanation of each)

"'Teacher, which commandment of the law is the greatest?' Jesus said to him, 'You shall love the Lord your God with your whole heart, with your whole soul, and with all your mind. This is the greatest and first commandment. The second is like it – You shall love your neighbor as yourself. On these two command-ments the whole law is based, and the prophets as well.'" (Matthew 22:36-40)

Is God bossy?

Why did God give us these commandments in the first place? Is He trying to tell us that He is the boss, and woe to us if we do not obey Him? Not at all. God gave us these commandments as a guide for our lives. If we obey them, our life will be much better, more enjoyable, and happier. Remember, too, that He also gave us a free will so that we can *choose* to obey Him or not to obey. Is God vengeful? Does God punish us if we do not obey His commandments? No, God does not punish us. Instead He lets us reap the consequences of our actions. What does that mean? Let's take an example:

Suppose you are a person who is allergic to strawberries. One day you go to your friend's house and he/she has a basket full of luscious red, ripe, just- picked strawberries. You are told to help yourself. So, you taste one, and it is so very good. What do you think will happen if you eat a number of them? Hives, itchy rash big time! It probably won't happen immediately, but tomorrow – not good. Well, that's sort of what happens when we don't keep God's laws. Our sin might not affect us immediately, or so it may seem, but sooner or later, it catches us with us. Then we suffer the consequences – the greater the sin, the more severe the consequences.

What is evil?

According to St. Thomas Aquinas, evil is the lack of good. Evil is not a thing in itself. It is the hurtful absence of what should be present. Evil is nonbeing and cannot be willed for its own sake. The will chooses good. Only when evil is masked as good, that is, when some good is perceived, can it be chosen.[4] In other words, a person will choose evil when he/she thinks there is some good to be derived from it.

Example: A teenage girl shoplifts a music CD from a store. The act is wrong, but the girl perceives the enjoyment she will get from listening to it. Therefore, she takes it. The first time she steals the CD is the hardest. She probably worries about getting caught knowing that it is wrong. If she gets away with it, she may decide to try it again. And so it goes, leading to more and perhaps bigger more expensive items. It could go on for years until she finally gets caught. Then come the tears, the remorse, the court trial, the jail sentence. Wow! Not a happy camper. Was it worth all the pain and suffering, the humiliation to herself and her family? What do you think?

How hard is it to follow God's laws?

"The love of God consists in this: that we keep His commandments – and His commandments are not burdensome." (1 John 5:3) It is really true that His commandments are not burdensome. Actually, they make life easier. They help us to *know* and better understand

---

[4] *A Tour of the Summa*, Msgr. Paul J. Glenn, p. 23

what will be beneficial in our life. So many times I have heard pastors, priests, and speakers tell us how hard it is to live for God, to follow His commandments. I have thought about this many times. Every time I have had to disagree with that premise and always came to the conclusion that it is much easier to follow God's commandments than not. The reason is that when you do something against God's laws, you usually end up with more trouble than you bargained for, and who needs that? For example, if you commit a criminal act such as rob a convenience store, you will get caught. Then you face criminal charges, a jail term, or whatever the punishment calls for, not to mention the humiliation. This may follow you for many years afterwards. If you are not caught, you still have to carry the burden of a guilty conscience. Not fun.

Another example would be a husband or wife who cheats on his/her spouse. First, there is the sneaking around and the guilt. When it is finally found out, and it always is, imagine all the pain caused to the spouse, the children, the family members, the humiliation in relation to friends. There could be a divorce – more pain, disruption of the family, custody battles, children being shuffled between parents for visitation rights, resentments, psychological scars, not to mention lawyers' fees. Messy business? You bet. And all this suffering never completely goes away. It may lessen over time, but it never really goes away. Why all this suffering? All because of someone's sin – the breaking of God's commandments.

Even smaller transgressions have their consequences. Telling even one lie can cause another to question that person's creditability in other matters. Many other examples can be given.

It all comes down to one conclusion: if you transgress the laws of God, sooner or later it catches up with you. You can end up with all kinds of problems and troubles. My Dad always said, "When you look for trouble, you find it." Who needs that? Think about that. Apply this kind of reasoning to your own situation, to your own life. Have you done something against God's guidelines? If so, what were the consequences? Did someone get hurt? Did you get hurt? Be completely honest with yourself. Don't be afraid. No one is going to question you. Ask God for forgiveness. Then decide whether there is something you can do to fix the problem, to make things better. Then do it. Seek forgiveness first from God, then from those whom you may have hurt. Sometimes the hurt is so deep that the other person may not be willing to forgive you. In that case, pray that God will soften his/her heart and in time that person may be able to forgive. And finally, forgive yourself and move on with your life.

Is it ever hard to follow God's laws?

There are some instances where you might say that living according to God's laws *is* hard. Living in a country where Christians and Jews are persecuted would seem to be a very difficult undertaking indeed. Joel C. Rosenberg in his book *Inside the Revolution* interviews a number of Muslims who have embraced Christianity. These people live in fear for their very lives from the authorities, from neighbors, and acquaintances, from friends, and even from their own family members. Amazingly these people live with much joy in their hearts. Having found love for Jesus gives them undaunted courage in the face of real danger. Mr. Rosenberg relates the following true story:

One man, a jihad cell commander, trained others to fight, plunder and kill "infidels." One day one of his disciples found someone distributing Bibles. He collected and destroyed all but one which he brought to his commander so that he could read it to learn how to react to it and counter it. It was a New Testament. The commander began to read it. He was looking for all the blasphemous rhetoric and corruption it supposedly contained. Instead, he found as he explained, "words of love, powerful words, not human words, God's words." He became deeply troubled, kept reading becoming intrigued by it. He had many questions, but no one to ask. He began comparing it with the Quran and began to beg God to show him the truth. And God did.

That night he had a dream in which he was standing amid a crowd watching a parade. In the parade he saw many prophets riding on horses coming toward the crowd. There was Jonah, David, Abraham, and Moses. Everyone kept cheering. He kept waiting for Muhammad to come riding by, but Muhammad never came. Finally, at the end of the procession a figure came riding a donkey. His face was covered. The commander asked, "Are you Jesus?" The Man pulled the cloth away from His face, smiled at him and nodded yes. The commander was filled with a joy he had never felt before in his entire life. When the commander awoke, he found his pillow wet from his tears. He realized that he had been so very wrong about God, about Jesus, about Islam, about terrorism. He became incredibly grateful and humbled that Jesus would come and rescue him and forgive all his sins. He became a devout and convincing evangelist. His murderous days were over and joy filled his heart.[5] The commander is a hunted man, and if he is ever caught, he faces torture and certain death. Read the entire story for yourself.

Many other Muslim-turned-Christian people face the same threat of torture and certain death if they are caught. Their joy at finding out the truth about God and His promise of eternal life far outweighs the consequences making it all worthwhile. If you happen to be a Muslim and are incredulous about all this, ask God Himself to reveal

---

5   *Inside the Revolution*, Joel C. Rosenberg, pp 453-458

His truth to you so you can decide for yourself. God is good and loving and will not steer you wrong.

Right now the question is: Do you want to know the truth? If your answer is "yes," then come along. If Jesus is the *truth* and no one comes to the Father except through Him, then doesn't it make sense to follow Him? On the other hand, if you are still skeptical, but curious, come along and see. If you really don't care, come along anyway just to see what happens. If your answer is "no," come along, too. You have nothing to lose by doing so. You, too, are most welcome.

Whatever your position, why not say this little prayer? It is non-denominational. If you are an atheist, say it anyway even if you don't believe it and it is only words to you. Be open to the truth whatever that may be just because you would like to know what *really is the truth*. Let the Holy Spirit lead you. Even if you don't believe that there is a Holy Spirit, **be open.** You may be surprised as to how things will turn out for you. All you need is a sincere heart and God will do the rest.

> **O Lord God Most High, Creator of the Universe, I want to know the truth. If You truly are, then help me to know it. Open my eyes that I may see the truth. Open my ears that I may hear the truth. Open my mind that I may understand the truth. Open my heart that I may embrace the truth. Help me to know that You truly love me. Help me to know what You desire of me that I may find happiness in You for now and for all eternity. Amen.**

How does God want us to love Him?

God wants us to love Him with our whole heart, with our whole soul, with our whole mind, and with all our strength. In other words, God wants us to put Him first in our life. He does not want us to put anyone or anything else in His place. God tells us, "I am the Lord, your God. . .you shall not have other gods before Me. You shall not carve idols in the shape of anything in the sky above or on the earth below or in the waters beneath the earth. You shall not bow down before them." (Exodus 20:2-5)

People in the days of the Old Testament did some of these things. While this may seem kind of ludicrous in this day and age, there are still some cultures that worship idols. But what about ordinary people like you and me? Do we worship false gods? Idolatry? Am I kidding? It is really surprising as to what are some of the false gods that we worship. How can that be? Some people worship other gods in the form of an inordinate desire for wealth, power, worldly possessions – that new luxury car that one can't really afford, or even another person whose every whim and fancy we follow. Isn't this a form of idolatry? We must worship God alone and trust Him alone.

Do some people put their trust in other than God? How about this: do you make use of spells and charms, believe in mediums (people who claim to converse with or contact the dead), witchcraft, sorcery, spiritists, fortunetellers? Are you superstitious? These things are all contrary to the first commandment of God. Why are they wrong? They are wrong and sinful because believing in them invests in them a power they do not and cannot have, a power that belongs to God alone. They really don't work. Don't fool yourself and waste your time and money paying for the services of charlatans and the like.

Who else do you love?

Before a person can love others, he/she must first love himself/herself. You need to look at yourself and take stock. To begin with, you need to remind yourself that you were created by a good and loving God. You are made in His image. No other creature on earth has that distinction of being made in God's image. Humankind alone has that special feature. Think about that. How wonderful!

The next thing you need to realize is that you are a unique, one-of-a-kind individual. There is no one else like you in this entire world. There never has been nor will there ever be anyone else *exactly* like you. Even if you are an identical twin, you and your twin are not exactly alike. That means that you are a very special person indeed.

As a baby needs his/her parents, each of us has a real need for our Father God who created us. In time a baby will grow to become an adult and probably no longer have a need for his/her parents for most concerns. However, you never outgrow your need for God. Without God we can do nothing. Without God we are nothing. Without God we would not even exist. If each person could fully realize his/her dependence on God, each would have more peace in life knowing that God has a special plan for each person. God has complete control over all things with the exception of your free will. Trusting God completely is the key to peace and happiness. When we allow God to handle every aspect of our life, we don't have to worry about anything. Hard to do? Yes, for most people; but it doesn't have to be that way. You can learn to trust God by reminding yourself that God loves you *unconditionally* and wants only the best for you. God wants you to be happy.

What do we mean by unconditional love?

God loves you unconditionally. That means that no matter what you look like, no matter who you are, no matter what you do even if you displease Him by your sins, God still loves you. He will always love you. You don't have to earn it; it is given to you freely. It is a gift. You don't have to be worthy or deserving of His love.

What about loving our neighbor?

Who is our neighbor? Every human person is made in God's image. Everyone is our neighbor, or more correctly, our brother or sister. Following God's commandments makes it so much easier to love others. How?

Learn to accept each person as he/she is. Since each person is unique, no two alike, there will, of course, be differences in the way each person sees and understands things. Cultures are different. Don't try to change a person into what you think he/she should be. Respect the likes and dislikes of others whether you agree with them or not. Avoid judging a person's words or actions. You have not "walked in their shoes;" therefore, you cannot know for certain what is in the heart. Only God knows that; leave the judging up to Him. We should avoid causing ill feelings and tension with one another. Being pleasant, courteous, and respectful of another makes for a much better relationship. If we have hurt someone, we need to apologize. Is it hard to apologize? Sometimes. But you can swallow your pride. Do it. You both will be much happier if you do. Trust me.

Don't be jealous of another person's accomplishments or possessions. This does you no good. If you harbor these feelings, you are the one who suffers. You are the one with the knot in your stomach. You are the one carrying around all the poison inside you. Poison? Yes, poison. These ill feelings literally poison your body. They are toxins to you and can cause all kinds of illnesses. Is that what you want? I doubt it. What can you do about it? Change your attitude. Learn to be happy for another's success. It will make a world of difference to you.

In order to build better relationships we need to share ourselves with others. Be willing to listen to their concerns, their fears and anxieties, their troubles. We should not try to tell others what to do, but rather offer suggestions as to what may help them. We should offer our services to them according to their needs. <u>Caution:</u> do not allow someone to take advantage of your loving nature. Some people will use others as a "doormat" to the point where resentment sets in. Learn to use good judgment in dealing with people. Don't let them become unnecessarily dependent on you. Don't become an enabler allowing them to get away with bad behavior. When you are in need, don't be afraid to ask for help. Be sure to express your gratitude for all that is done for you.

How can one learn to be happy?

The most important thing you can do for yourself is to accept yourself as you are. Learn to count your blessings and be grateful to God for all that He has given you and all that He has done for you. Take good care of yourself and those you love. If there is something about yourself that you don't like, take steps to change it. Learn to see the good in yourself and other people. Don't blame others for your shortcomings. Educate yourself. Learn something new – take classes, grow. Learn to relax; don't be a workaholic. Learn to enjoy people for who they are, not for who you want them to be. Who has time for all this? You don't have to do everything. Choose what is best for you. Be flexible. Learn to enjoy life.

And, oh yes, one more thing – take time to pray, to be with God. He is the source of your strength and happiness. With God's help you can accomplish all kinds of things for yourself and for others. Make your whole life an act of love. You will be amazed at all the good things you will find in your life. **You will be happy!**

Love is patient; love is kind.
Love is not jealous; does not put on airs;
It is not snobbish. Love Is never rude;
it is not self-seeking;
It is not prone to anger; neither does it brood over injustices.

Love does not rejoice in what is wrong
But rejoices with the truth.
There is no limit to love's forbearance,
To its trust, its hope, its power to endure. Love never fails.

There are in the end three things that last:
Faith, hope, and love, and
the greatest of these is love.

(1 Corinthians 13:4-8, 13)

II

The Good, the Bad, the Ugly, and the Irredeemable?

Chapter 1

The Good: Who Are They?

"There is some good in the worst of us and some evil in the best of us. When we discover this, we are less prone to hate our enemies."
Dr. Martin Luther King, Jr.

Are there really good people?

Of course, there are good people. Everyone knows that. Who are they? These are the people who always put God first in their life and other people before themselves – even to the point of risking their own life. This brings to mind our Police, Firefighters, Military, First Responders, and others who daily put their life on the line to protect and save others. Jesus said, "There is no greater love than this: to lay down one's life for one's friends." (John 15;13)

Is it necessary to give up one's life?

You don't have to literally die to give up your life for others. Living for others can more than fill the bill. Let's take some examples:

<u>Mother Teresa of Calcutta, India</u> was a Catholic nun who ministered to the poorest of the poor. She founded the community of nuns known as the Missionaries of Charity. In spite of great opposition, she

When Good Things Happen to Bad People

opened a facility for the sick and dying people of Calcutta welcoming all regardless of their beliefs. The sisters of her community would tend to the dying person with the attitude that he/she, made in the image and likeness of God, is valued and respected interpreting death as a means of "finding God again" not as an opportunity for conversion to Catholicism. "They respect the beliefs – and the unbelief – of all those who come here. For example the sisters will sprinkle the dying Hindu with water from the Ganges River, read a passage from the Koran to the dying Moslem, and observe the appropriate rites of death with the Christian."[6]

Mother Teresa ministered to the poorest of the poor and lived as they did. Why? She was a well-educated woman, a teacher, an intelligent woman. She could have done so much else with her life. Why did she give all that up to go to Calcutta, India to live in poverty among the diseased and dying people? She did it for the love of God and the love of people. How many of us could do that?

Mother Teresa received the Nobel Peace Prize in 1979 among 18 international awards for her humanitarian work. She died on September 5, 1997 at the age of 87. Pope John Paul II, who is now a canonized saint in the Catholic Church, beatified her on October 19, 2003. Pope Francis canonized her as Saint Teresa of Calcutta on September 4, 2016.

Martin Luther King, Jr. was an American Baptist minister and activist leader in the Civil Rights Movement. He Promoted civil rights through peaceful demonstrating nonviolence and civil disobedience based on his religious Christian beliefs. Rev. King led the 1955 Montgomery bus boycott and helped found the Southern Christian Leadership Conference in 1957. He organized nonviolent protests

---

6   *Mother Teresa: Her Life, Her Work, Her Message*, Jose Luis Gonzalez-Balado, p. 70

in Birmingham, Alabama in 1963 and the March on Washington where he delivered his famous speech, "I Have a Dream." In October 1964, he received the Nobel Peace Prize for his work in racial inequality through nonviolent resistance. Continuing his work, Rev. King helped to organize the Selma to Montgomery marches, worked on segregated housing in Chicago, on opposition towards poverty, and the Vietnam War.

In 1968 Rev. King was in the process of planning the Poor People's Campaign for Washington, D.C. when he was assassinated by James Earl Ray on April 4 in Memphis, Tennessee. This caused riots in many cities across the U.S. Ray fled the country and was arrested two months later at London Heathrow Airport. He was sentenced to 99 years in prison for the murder of Martin Luther King, Jr.

The Presidential Medal of Freedom and the Congressional Medal were posthumously awarded to Rev. King. Martin Luther King, Jr. Day was made a federal holiday in 1986 and the Martin Luther King, Jr. Memorial on the National Mall In Washington, D.C. was dedicated in 2011.[7] Rev. Martin Luther King, Jr. actually gave up his life for his cause of promoting the civil rights of all people especially African-Americans through nonviolence.

What about the rest of us?

There are good people who dedicate their very life to helping other people. These are the saintly people who most definitely work their way to a place reserved for them in heaven. What about you and me? Most of us have our family to care for, our job to provide for our needs, the everyday chores – grocery shopping, preparing meals, laundry, getting the kids off to school, sports events, other activities, fixing the broken appliances, etc. We *need* to take care of these things.

---

[7] Martin Luther King, Jr., Wikipedia, the free encyclopedia

We are unable to dedicate our entire life to helping many other people as did Mother Teresa or Rev. King. We can, however, get involved in activities designed to help people in need such as volunteering at charitable events, helping with Meals on Wheels, serving in soup kitchens, helping with fund raising, visiting nursing homes and hospitals, helping a neighbor in need. Most of us work our way to heaven by means of these smaller, but still important endeavors. Does God pay attention to these little kindnesses? You bet He does! Will our reward also be in heaven? Absolutely!

Did you ever have to make a really hard decision?

At our church, Father Jack, a former pastor, during his homily told this true story:

Three men, a father, a son, and his son's friend were out on a large lake in a small boat when a rather violent storm came up tossing the boat perilously on the waves. The boat capsized and the men were thrown into the water. The father was able to grab onto the boat and secure a rope. Now he had to make a very difficult choice – to whom should he throw the rope, to his son or to his son's friend? He reasoned. He knew that his son was a good person and walked with the Lord. If he died, his son would surely have salvation and be with God for eternity. On the other hand, he had no knowledge of the state of the soul of the friend. If the friend died, would he have salvation? Not knowing the answer, the father threw the rope to the son's friend and was able to save him. Unfortunately, his own son perished in the water and his body was never found.

The story was told by an elderly priest who was celebrating the Mass with a young priest. After Mass two young persons came up to the old priest and said that they had a hard time believing such a story. It was then that the old priest revealed that he was the father who had made that most difficult decision and the young priest was his son's friend whom he had saved.

What a difficult decision to make. It takes courage to do what you are afraid to do. You need to conquer your fear. Can you do that? Yes, with God's help you can.

What is heaven like?

Heaven, supposedly, is the place where all the good people go after they die. How do we know about heaven and what it is like? As you well know, the source of all knowledge is God, and God speaks to us through Sacred Scripture. "Indeed, we know that when the earthly tent (our body) in which we dwell is destroyed, we have a dwelling provided by God, a dwelling in the heavens, not made by hands but to last forever." (Corinthians 5:1) This tells us that our soul is immortal, and God's plan is for us to be happy with Him for all eternity. Heaven is a reward for living according to God's laws and for performing good deeds. We are created for love and friendship, for a joyful and everlasting reunion with our family and friends after death in heaven. All religions adhere to the belief in some sort of heaven.

Scripture tells us that in heaven we will see God face to face. This is the greatest happiness that God intends us to have. God is an infinite being. His grandeur is unknown to us while we are on earth. Our ability to have a personal relationship with Him is very limited. What will our relationship be like in heaven? "Our relationship with God will be that of a very personal intimacy and friendship, a truly mutual and reciprocal love and affection. In God there is no condescension which would kill the friendship...He is the Creator and they are the creatures...There is no need of an effort to make a show of superiority towards one's own handiwork. Hence, God can embrace

His creature with infinite abandonment of love, and the creature can respond to the utmost of its capacity."[8]

There is always happiness and eternal rest and peace. There is no pain or sadness in heaven where every tear will be wiped away. "He shall wipe every tear from their eyes, and there shall be no more death or mourning, crying out in pain, for the former world has passed away." (Revelation 21:4) The blessed souls in heaven are in perfect harmony with God's Divine Will; therefore, they can no longer sin. They do feel displeasure at the sins of the people on earth, but without experiencing any real pain. They greatly delight in being in the company of Jesus, Mary, the angels, and all the saints, and in reunion of all those who were dear to them on earth. A special source of joy will be the union of the soul with the resurrected glorified body which will be like the glorified body of Jesus Christ after He rose from the dead. According to the definition by the Council of Florence, there are various degrees of beatitude or blessedness corresponding to the various degrees of merit acquired by the individual soul while on earth. The Bible teaches this truth in many passages whenever it speaks of eternal happiness as a reward.[9]

What is the Beatific Vision?

In heaven, the blessed will directly see the very essence of God. "We shall see Him as He is." (1 John 3:2) This is called the Beatific Vision. However, no creature can know God completely as the finite cannot possibly know the infinite entirely. The happiness that we experience will be according to the merit we have achieved while on earth. Yet, each soul will be completely happy and have a full measure of satisfaction according to his/her own capacity. This is determined by the

---

8   *Purgatory and Heaven*, J.P. Arendzen, D.D., pp. 63-65
9   "Heaven," Catholic Encyclopedia

love of God and of neighbor that he/she exhibited while on earth. While on earth we may have a few really happy moments where we are really satisfied; but these moments are always fleeting. They never last. We have certain cravings or longings for something that we do not yet possess. Will we have any cravings or longings in heaven? Not at all – we will always be completely satisfied. The happiness of one saint may be greater than that of another, but each will be completely filled to his/her capacity.

Heaven will always be fresh. Its beauty cannot be described in earthly terms. We will gaze in amazement at all the loveliness that we perceive, and there is no end to it. The novelty will never wear off. God says, "Behold, I make all things new." (Revelations 21:5)

All this is reassuring to know that in heaven we will be eternally happy. Do we have to take all this on faith alone? Is there anyone who has actually seen what heaven is like – maybe just a little glimpse of heaven? Believe it or not, there are numerous accounts of people who have had a glimpse of heaven through visions or near-death experiences. Most of the time these people have been reluctant to talk about it because the experience has proven to be indescribable and so incredible that they feared they would not be believed. Others would think that they were dreaming, imagining things, or just plain crazy.

St. Faustina Kowalska (1905-1938) a Polish nun, was given the privilege to have a glimpse of heaven about which she wrote in her diary on page 592, "Incomprehensible is the happiness in which the soul will be immersed." She goes on to write on page 777, ". . .I was in heaven, in spirit, and I saw its inconceivable beauties and the happiness that awaits us after death. This source of happiness is unchanging in its essence, but is always new, gushing forth happiness for all creatures. Now I understand Saint Paul who said, 'Eye has not seen, nor has ear heard, nor has it entered into the heart of man what God has prepared for those who love Him.'" (1 Corinthians 2:9)

What is death? Is it scary?

Death is when the soul leaves the body. It is a very natural happening. Everybody dies at some time. The reason that it is frightening for some people is the fear of the unknown. Some people believe that when a person dies, that is the end; there is nothing more. How sad that would be. When you really think about death, reason tells you that there has to be something more. I mean why would God create us only to have us go into nothingness in the end? That doesn't make much sense. Some people have actually died and have come back to life and were able to tell us about their experience.

What happens when a person dies?

According to those who have had a near-death experience, an extremely bright light is perceived. That light is usually another being – like an angel. Some see Jesus, the Son of God. Great peace is felt with an all-enveloping warmth. The joy of knowing a completely unconditional love regardless of who you are is overwhelming. Indescribable is the splendor and beauty as is the heavenly music, not at all like the noise we call music here on earth. Blessed spirits including family members and friends who have gone before you come to greet you with much joy. And remember that this is only a small glimpse of the glory and all the wonderful surprises that await us in the hereafter. Does any of this sound scary to you? I doubt it. It sounds wonderful to me.

The Good: Who Are They?

Would you like a glimpse of heaven?

Following are some accounts of people who have had a glimpse of heaven. These are not canonized saints, just ordinary people like you and me:

Don Piper – In January 1989, an ordinary Baptist minister was on his way back from a conference when he was involved in a head-on collision with an eighteen-wheeler truck. His small car was totaled and he was pronounced dead at the scene. Another Baptist preacher came upon the accident and insisted on praying for Don even though the EMTs told him that it was too late. This preacher prayed for 90 minutes. His prayers were answered, and Don came back to life. Because of his extensive injuries, he had a long road to recovery. Don gives us an account of the experience that completely changed his life. However, for our purposes we will focus on his 90 minutes in the land of the dead.

Don explains that he did not go through a dark tunnel. A brilliant light beyond description enveloped him, and he found himself standing in heaven. He saw a large crowd of people, some of whom he knew – all of them smiling and praising God. He saw his grandfather who embraced him. Many others welcomed him and he felt very much loved. He saw many friends and relatives. There was so much warmth and radiant light, vivid dazzling colors far surpassing anything he had ever seen – incomprehensible beauty. The music was the most beautiful he had ever heard, and he was completely embraced by joyous sounds. All this was just before he was to step through the gates. He was never in the presence of God. He states that, "...once we're actually in God's presence, we will never return to earth again, because it will be empty and meaningless by comparison." Then suddenly, Don found himself back in his body.[10]

It might be well to note at this point that those who have had a near-death experience and have had a glimpse of heaven tell of their unwillingness to return to their body. They wanted to stay in heaven. So why did they come back? They were told that they needed to complete a particular mission here on earth or that their time had not yet come. So reluctantly they found themselves back in their body.

One thing I can't understand – why would anyone want to risk losing all the wonder and beauty of heaven by not believing in God or by not following His commandments? How foolish is that? How about you? Would you want to risk losing heaven? Not me.

There are many scientists that have argued that near-death experiences are impossible. Are they?

Dr. Eben Alexander – a highly-trained neurosurgeon was such a person. He knew that these experiences feel real, but he believed that they are simply fantasies produced by brains under stress. His neuroscience knowledge could not allow him to comprehend a belief in God, heaven, or even a soul. Then mysteriously Dr. Alexander contracted a rare brain illness. The part of his brain that controls thought and emotion shut down completely and put him in a coma for seven days. His doctors considered stopping treatment when suddenly his eyes popped open. His recovery was considered a medical miracle. There is much more to his story. Dr. Alexander states, "But now that I have been privileged to understand that life does not end with the

---

10   *90 Minutes in Heaven,* Don Piper, p. 33, Guideposts, Carmel, New York, 2004

THE GOOD: WHO ARE THEY?

death of the body or the brain, I see it my duty, my calling, to tell people about what I saw beyond the body and beyond this earth."[11]

While in the state of a coma, Dr. Alexander at first found himself in a murky darkness like transparent mud with grotesque animal faces and terrifyingly weird sounds. There were reptilian, wormlike creatures and a smell like feces, blood, and vomit. Could this have been hell? Then something beautiful happened. It appeared in the darkness radiating fine filaments of white-gold light. The darkness splintered and broke apart. There was the most beautiful music that obliterated the terrifying sounds. The doctor then found himself in the "strangest, most beautiful world I'd ever seen. . .A beautiful, incredible dream world. . .I was absolutely sure of one thing: this place I'd suddenly found myself in was completely real."[12] He encountered many luminous beings full of joy.

Dr. Alexander continued moving forward and entered an immense void, pitch black, but brimming over with light coming from a brilliant living Orb which turned out to be God, the Creator – the unconditionally loving God. The doctor was "told that there is not one universe but many. . .but that love lay at the center of them all. Evil was present in all the other universes as well. . .Evil was necessary because without it free will was impossible, and without free will could be no growth – no chance for us to become what God longed for us to be. . .love was overwhelmingly dominant, and it would ultimately be triumphant."[13]

Mary C. Neal, MD tells us "Without observing cruelty, we would not be moved to compassion. Without personal trials, we would not

---

11   *Proof of Heaven A Neurosurgeon's Journey into the Afterlife,* Eban Alexander, M.D., p. 10, Simon & Schuster, New York, NY
12   Ibid, pp. 38-39
13   Ibid, pp. 47-48

develop patience or faithfulness. . .our earthly concerns matter little when compared to life eternal that allows us to know joy in the midst of sorrow and worry."[14]

"I understood that I was part of the Divine and that nothing – absolutely nothing – could ever take that away. The (false) suspicion that we can somehow be separated from God is the root of anxiety in the universe, and the cure for it. . .was the knowledge that nothing can tear us away from God, ever."[15]

Back to Dr. Alexander – he was probably a good person even though he did not believe in God, heaven, or the existence of the soul. God, however, truly loves us and knows how to reach us. His love for each person is so great that He will go to unimaginable lengths to save us and to bring us to Himself. After all, look what Jesus, the Son of God, did for us in His life, crucifixion, death, and resurrection so that we could have eternal life. The good doctor was shown the truth that he may believe and have salvation. Did this make a big change in his life? You better believe it. Can God make a big difference in your life? You better believe that, too!

Heaven through the eyes of a child?

Colton Burpo was not yet four years old when Reverend Todd Burpo, Pastor of Crossroads Wesleyan Church in Imperial, Nebraska was taking his family on a trip. Colton suddenly became very sick. He was taken immediately to the hospital and after many tests, it was determined that Colton needed immediate surgery.

Many prayers went up for Colton and he made what was considered a miraculous recovery and was able to go home.

---

14   *To Heaven And Back*, Mary C. Neal, MD, Waterback Press, Division of Random House, New York, p. 100

15   Ibid, p. 76

The Good: Who Are They?

Then many strange things began to happen. Colton began to tell of his having almost died during the surgery. He told of how he went up out of his body, up to heaven, having spoken with angels, and having sat in Jesus' lap.

Colton described what heaven was like. He told his Dad amazing things in words that only a four-year old could describe, things that matched Sacred Scripture in every detail.

Read for yourself the incredible true story of a very young child who saw and described what heaven is like. In his book, *Heaven is for Real*, Todd Burpo relates the entire account of what Colton experienced, what he saw in heaven, who he met there, and how he knew past unbelievable family occurrences that he could not possibly have known beforehand.

Colton also mentioned that there are lots of kids in heaven as well as animals.

You can obtain this book, *Heaven is for Real*, which is Published in Nashville, Tennessee by Thomas Nelson, a registered trademark of Thomas Nelson, Inc.

For more information you can go to an email at SpecialMarkets@ThomasNelson.com. *Heaven is for Real* has become a #1 New York Times Best Seller with over two million copies in print.

The book has also been made into a movie and is on DVD. You can obtain both the book and the DVD, *Heaven is for Read* on Amazon.com. The true story is absolutely amazing. Check it out. I highly recommend reading it which has more explicit details than does the DVD.

Why do some people see heaven?

Why are some people from the time of the Old Testament days until the present day favored with a glimpse of heaven? I believe that the reason is so that they could relate this incredible information to the rest of us who have not seen so that we may believe.

How about you? Do you still not believe or have some questions in your mind? Are you still wary of all this? Don't let your doubts haunt you. Do yourself a huge favor – check out these stories for yourself. If you don't want to read the Bible where God Himself tells you, then read some of the books written by or about people who have had these experiences.

A marvelous book put out by Guideposts is *Discover the Secrets of Heaven* which gives a number of such accounts. *Return from Tomorrow* by George G. Ritchie, *90 Minutes in Heaven* by Don Piper, *Heaven is for Real* by Todd Burpo, *Proof of Heaven* by Eban Alexander, M.D. will leave you awestruck and filled with wonder. Amazon.com is a great place to find almost any book. While you are at it, also Google Life After Death and Near-Death Experiences.

Will all people get to heaven eventually?

No. There are those people whose lives are so corrupt that they will never get to see the glories of heaven. However, I believe that most people will *eventually* get to heaven for three reasons:

> First, God is all merciful and loves each one of his children unconditionally. He gives each person the graces needed to get to heaven. He constantly pursues us because His love is so great. God does not want any of His children to be lost. The choice to accept His grace is up to each person. Remember we have free will. *Each individual person gets to choose* where he/she will end up for all eternity.
>
> Second, the Son of God, in the person of Jesus Christ, came down from heaven, became one of us to teach us how to live. He taught us how to be kind and compassionate, merciful and forgiving, patient, and to love one another as God loves each one of

us. Through His excruciating suffering, death on the cross, and resurrection He paid the price for our sins in order that we may have eternal life with Him in heaven. What a hollow victory it would be if only few people were to attain heaven.

Third, God gives us many means of help which we will discuss in Section III – Why Suffering & Why Forgiveness? of this book. God wants the salvation of as many of His children as possible.

Do all dogs go to heaven?

There is a popular movie entitled *All Dogs Go To Heaven*. Do they? Do any of our beloved pets go to heaven? Will we see them there? Some people believe that we will indeed be united with our furry friends who never asked for anything but to be loved. Some of these furry friends have faced dangers and have even given their life for their owner. As a girl in grade school I remember being told that animals have a mortal soul that dies when the animal dies. Is that the case? How sad that would be. Does anyone know the answer? Eileen George sheds some light on this mystery.

First of all, who is Eileen George? Eileen, who passed away on May 14, 2017 at the age of 90, was an ordinary person like you and me – a wife, mother, grandmother. She was chosen by God the Father to bring a special message to all people. The message is that God is our *real* Father Who is loving, caring, and gentle, and Who wants to be part of every aspect of our life. She has spoken all over the world to thousands of people. She had a healing ministry and is recognized by good Christian people including a number of Roman Catholic Bishops. I have personally seen and heard her speak at least three times. She always left her audience with a feeling of peace and the knowledge of God's great love for each person. There is no question that her words were always based on solid teaching and traditions according to Jesus Christ.

Eileen at one time had a beautiful black horse, a stallion named Midnight. She was quite a horsewoman and had won many ribbons with Midnight. She loved that horse. As time went by, Midnight became old and was dying. Eileen cried and begged God not to take him away from her. However, it was not to be – Midnight died. Eileen became angry with God. She said, "I asked You to give Midnight life and You gave him death." God replied, "No child. I gave him real life. When you finally turn that doorknob of death, he will be in your valley. You asked me to give him life, I gave him real life." Midnight was waiting for her in heaven. Eileen went on to explain, "Did the horse earn heaven? No. But I'm earning heaven by grace and acceptance of grace and God will give me everything my heart desires including my beloved black stallion, Midnight. . .The horse doesn't earn heaven, we do, and God gives us everything outside of sin that our heart desires."[16] Eileen must surely be enjoying her reunion with her beloved Midnight in her heavenly valley.

Speaking of horses, when little four-year old Colton Burpo was playing with his toys, he picked up a plastic horse and said, "Hey, Dad, did you know that Jesus has a horse?" Todd replied, "A horse?" Colton continued, "Yeah, a rainbow horse. I got to pet him. There's lots of colors."[17]

According to Eileen George and little Colton Burpo, your favorite pet will be waiting for you in heaven.

How wonderful! How Great!

---

16   *Eileen George: Beacon of God's Love: Her Teaching*, pp. 175-176, The Meeting-the-Father Ministry, Inc., Millbury, Massachusetts

17   *Heaven is for Real*, Todd Burpo, p. 63, Thomas Nelson, Inc., Nashville, Tennessee, 2010

The Good: Who Are They?

<u>God Made Us A Family</u>

We need one another
We love one another
We forgive one another
We work together
We play together
We worship together

Together we use God's word
Together we grow in Christ
Together we love all people
Together we serve our God
Together we hope for heaven
These are our hopes and ideals.

Help us to attain them, O God.
Through Jesus Christ our Lord.

Maryknoll Fathers and Brothers
Catholic Foreign Mission Society of America, Inc.
MaryknollSociety.org

For God so loved the world
That He have His only Son,
That whoever believes in Him
Should not perish
But have eternal life.
John 3:16

<u>I Said a Prayer for You Today</u>

I know God must have heard.
I felt the answer in my heart
Although He spoke no word.
I didn't ask for wealth or fame,
I knew you wouldn't mind,
I asked Him to send treasures
Of a far more lasting kind.
I asked that He be near you
At the start of each new day,
To grant you health and blessings
And friends to share the way.
I asked for happiness for you
In all things great and small,
But it was for His loving care
I prayed for most of all.
(Frank Zamboni)

The same everlasting Father
Who cares for you today
Will care for you tomorrow
And every day.

Either He will shield you from suffering
Or give you unfailing strength to bear it.

Be at peace then and put aside
All anxious thoughts and imaginings.
(St. Francis de Sales)

Chapter 2

The Bad: How Bad Are We?

How bad is bad?

No one is perfect. Only God is perfect. As humans go, only Jesus and His Mother Mary were never tainted by sin. Since Jesus is God, the Second person of the Holy Trinity, He is sinless. His Mother Mary was given a special grace and privilege known as the Immaculate Conception. This means that from the very first instant of her conception in her mother's womb, she was free from original sin that is passed down to every person from Adam. This privilege was given to Mary because God had chosen her to be the mother of the Messiah, Jesus the incarnate Son of God. All the rest of us come into being with the stain of original sin on our soul. This is taken away through Baptism. I guess that means that there is a little bad in each of us. The rest of the bad comes to us by the choices we make using our free will. Some people choose bad things like saying nasty things about another person, telling lies, taking a small item that does not belong to them. Others commit more serious bad acts like shoplifting from a store, breaking and entering someone's home to rob them, assault and battery of another person, and other crimes that are punishable by law.

How does God see these people?

Does God love all these people who commit small sins a little less than the good people? Does God reject those who commit really bad acts until they wise up and turn their life around? No. God loves all His children unconditionally. That means that God loves you no matter who you are, whatever the color of your skin or sexual orientation, religious affiliation or lack thereof, where you come from, or what kind of trouble you may have caused. He always has and He always will. God never rejects anyone no matter the circumstances. Are you having a hard time believing that because you have done some bad things in your life? Not to worry. God loves you and will never abandon you. All you need to do is to call out to Him with a sincere heart. He is there for you. Believe it; it is true. Pray to Him. Ask Him. Trust Him. If you are unsure about this, try it – not to test God, but with sincerity and a wanting to reach out to God and see what happens.

What will God do?

God has the most amazing ways of reaching out to people. Why? Simply because of His great love for us. In Chapter 1 of this Section, we saw how God reached out to people through good people like Mother Teresa. God wanted us to know about heaven and some of the wonders He has planned for us so He tells us through some people who have had incredible near-death experiences. He reaches out to us through the caring of family, friends, and neighbors. But what about those people who deliberately cause trouble? Does God really care about them? How does He reach out to them? Let's see.

St. Augustine of Hippo in his young years was what we might call a "bad dude." He got into all kinds of mischief. He ran around with a "street gang" that got into stealing just for the fun of it. He got

The Bad: How Bad Are We?

involved in impure sexual habits. Augustine was a brilliant student, so his father who was a pagan ignored his son's reprehensible escapades as long as he did well in his studies. All this while his mother Monica's heart bled with anguish and many tears. She prayed for her son and her husband for something like twenty years. After many years, Monica's husband was finally converted and baptized about a year before he died.[18]

But what about her son, Augustine? Well he was still on the loose. He continued to get into more and more perverse activities. He became a slave to his sexual sins. He even fathered an illegitimate son whom his mother ended up raising like many of today's grandparents who are raising their grandchildren because their son or daughter got himself/herself into a mess and did not live up to his/her responsibilities. But what about Augustine? Wait it gets better, or should I say worse. He continued his studies and joined a heretical sect called the Manichees. Pride urged him on, and he scoffed at the teachings of the Church. "The grief of Monica at the fall of her gifted son into heresy was inexpressible. She prayed, and wept, and admonished. She regarded him as worse than a heathen...she forbade him to eat at her table, or even to enter her door."[19] Wow! Talk about tough love!

God hung on to Augustine and s-l-o-w-l-y led him to the truth. And all through this, Augustine was still chained to his sexual indiscretions. He began to humble himself before God. "He was chained down; but he wept and cried to Heaven."[20] Finally, to the great joy of his mother, he was converted and was baptized. Augustine became a priest, a bishop, and wrote prolifically. Best known of all works are *Confessions* where he pours out his heart confessing all his transgres-

---

18 *Little Lives of the Great Saints,* John O'Kane Murray, p. 218
19 Ibid, p. 218
20 Ibid, p. 219

sions and his anguish of soul, and *The City of God* which is a profound defense of the Christian religion. He is a Doctor of the Church. The oldest city in the United States, St. Augustine, Florida, is named after him.

St. Mary of Egypt was a prostitute. At the tender age of twelve, Mary left home and went to Alexandria where she led a life of public prostitution for over seventeen years. When she was about thirty years old, there was a pilgrimage going to Jerusalem for the feast of the Exaltation of the Holy Cross. She decided to go, but not for the intention of the pilgrimage, rather she went to seek new opportunities to gratify her insatiable lust. Upon arriving in Jerusalem, she continued her shameful life by seducing quite a number of men.

On the feast of the Exaltation of the Holy Cross, she joined the crowds hoping to gather more new victims whom she might lure into sin. When she reached the door of the church, she felt herself repelled by some strange force. She tried three or four times to enter the church but was unable to do so. Realizing that her wicked life was the reason for her rejection, filled with remorse, she burst into tears. Near the spot where she was standing she saw a statue of the Blessed Virgin Mary. She began to pray and begged the Blessed Virgin to intercede for her and obtain forgiveness from God. She promised to give up her sinful life. After her prayers, she felt encouraged and again approached the church to once more to try to enter. She found that she was easily able to enter the church. Mary venerated the Holy Cross and from then on changed her life. She went into the desert and lived apparently on herbs. She lived alone for forty-seven years praying and doing penance for her sins. While there, she met Zosimus, a priest and monk, who would from time to time bring her the Holy Eucharist. God is all loving and forgiving. He reaches out to what some might call the worst of society. The Greek Church celebrates

The Bad: How Bad Are We?

the feast of St. Mary of Egypt on April 1.[21] God sometimes uses the most unconventional means to reach us. Does it really work? You bet it does! Check out this next true modern-day story.

<u>Sister Mary Angelina</u> is a Catholic nun. The Catholic Charismatic Conference that is held every year the first weekend in August is where I listened to Sister Mary Angelina give her testimony. She was bright, funny, full of life, and beaming with an undeniably happy smile. Would anyone ever suspect that not too many years ago she struggled to reveal a deep dark secret in her life? It was a secret that kept her in bondage for many years.

Going through some old photos and papers at an early age, she learned that she had been adopted. Her biological parents had conceived her out of wedlock. Being rather young, they were unable to care for a baby. They decided to do what was best for the baby and gave her up for adoption. Her adoptive parents hid the truth from her that she was adopted, and when she learned of it, they advised her not to tell anyone as "some people might not be willing to understand." She felt that something was wrong and she felt rejected by her biological parents.

Even though her adoptive parents were good to her and did love her, she felt that no one truly loved her.

Then it happened. She was sexually abused. Sister did not give any details as to who had done this to her or how often it happened. She only explained the tremendous devastation it caused in her life. She felt used and unloved. Her innocence was taken from her. She was unable to tell anyone, not even her parents. She kept it a secret known only to herself.

---

21 *"St. Mary of Egypt," The Catholic Encyclopedia,* Vol. 9, Robert Appleton Company, New York

As a teenager she was not comfortable and always considered herself to be unattractive, awkward, and had longed for someone to care about her and love her. Friends did not last long. She began sneaking out at night, partying, drinking, and getting involved in sexual relationships because she wanted to be liked by other people. Not following her parents' rules and not trusting her friends only brought her sadness, never any lasting happiness.

As a college school student, she worked hard and wanted to be a successful business person. She wanted to be rich and famous. She wanted to meet many influential people and really make something of herself. Sister Mary Angelina was an intelligent woman. She began to pursue her career by getting involved in various activities. However, her lifestyle left much to be desired. By the time she was in her early twenties, she was already an alcoholic, did too much partying, and began using men and being used by them. In reality, she was a very unhappy person. Her pain, however, was known only to herself.

Was she a "bad" person? Was she evil? No. She was sick and unable to heal herself. She wanted to stop but couldn't face the deep pain that drove her addiction. Addiction is a manifestation or symptom of a deeper sorrow. As a young girl, she became the victim of sexual abuse. She kept this dark secret from her parents, from everyone. There was no one to rescue her or to protect her. She became angry at God for allowing this to happen to her. Sexual abuse can cause a person to feel shame, guilt, depression, self-hatred, lead to substance abuse, promiscuity, and other kinds of distress. Her response to her abuse was to become an alcoholic, to sexually use men and allow men to sexually use her. She buried her anger and resentment which led to chronic depression and shame.

How could she possibly be helped? Sister Mary Angelina did not grow up knowing that she was created in the image and likeness of

God. She did not know of God's unconditional love for every one of His children. She did not understand God as her loving Father or that He even cared about her. Sister led a life serving mostly herself. Her life of selfishness was not very happy. There was no peace and tranquility. What was it that Sister Mary Angelina needed? She needed to be healed of the feeling of abandonment by her biological parents. She needed to be healed of the hatred she had of her abuser. She needed to be healed of self-hatred and shame that kept her in bondage for years. And she needed to be healed of the feeling of being abandoned by God. How could all this be healed?

God ministers to the pain and sorrow in our hearts *through other people*. When we allow God into our hearts, freedom emerges from His presence. God never abandons us. He is always with us; we are never alone. Allow Jesus into your anguish. Pray, hope, and trust Him and He *will* heal you.

A very holy Catholic priest knew that Sister Mary Angelina's life had been sinful and broken. However, he did not see the shame. He saw her beauty and encouraged her to seek a life with God rather than waste her life in sin. She entered religious life and in her later twenties still felt immense brokenness and unhappiness. She needed to change. But how? She struggled with self-hatred, clinical depression, and felt very alone. Then through the kindness of many helpful people her life began to change. She learned of interior healing through a loving and caring sister in her community.

She was encouraged her to seek counseling to aid her healing. Several counselors spent many hours with her, never judging her reprehensible behavior. She felt accepted in recovery groups even though it was painful for her to face her feelings.

Sister had the opportunity to spend time with a family. She decided to take advantage of the chance to learn what a truly loving family would be like. She observed the love between a husband and a wife and how this kind of love affected their children.

The family continued to show their love by reaching out to other people who needed healing in their suffering. True love is not found in the absence of suffering but in the willingness to help one another through times that are demanding and difficult.

As a young girl, Sister did not have a very good relationship with her mother who was appalled at her lifestyle. As is the case with many young people, Sister Mary Angelina would not listen to her mother and insisted on following her own agenda. During her college years, her mother was so displeased with her daughter's sinful life that she reprimanded her, cut her off financially, and threatened to disown her. Sister remained head-strong and rebellious and refused to be told what to do. What she didn't know was that her mother had been doing a lot of praying over those years.

After Sister professed her first vows as a religious, her mother wished to talk with her. She explained that one night she prayed to the Blessed Mother and entrusted her rebellious, disobedient daughter to the care and protection of Mary the Mother of Jesus Christ. (See Appendix B – Mary the Mother of God) Her mother continued to pray that her daughter would enter the religious life. Since then mother and daughter have been on their own journey together of reconciliation and healing. Sister Mary Angelina now knows that she is loved by her adoptive mother, by other loving people, and most of all by God.

Yes, God in His great love and mercy brings healing to all who need it in His unique and surprising ways usually through the kindness and compassion of other people. He turns pain and suffering into joy and happiness. When I saw Sister Mary Angelina at the

The Bad: How Bad Are We?

Conference some years ago, she most definitely was filled with joy and happiness as she told her story.

What a wonderful and loving God we have. Don't you think so?

A soldier lay dying. When did this happen? Who was this soldier? It happened during World War II. He was a Russian soldier mortally wounded with only a few minutes left of his life. Was he a "bad" person? Did he live a life of sin? Did he know anything about God? Did he care about knowing God? We don't know. We don't know anything more about him or even his name. All we know is that he was dying. Did anyone care? Did God even care? *God always cares.* He loves all His children. God had a plan for this unfortunate soldier. God had put His plan for this soldier into motion a number of years before.

God's plan started in a small village in Czechoslovakia. Anne Marie Schmidt was a young girl who lived in this quiet obscure village. There was not much there. They had a Catholic church in the little community around which most of their activity centered. Anne Marie always knew that she was a child of God. One day while they were having Mass, a group of Nazi soldiers entered the church and threatened the people. The people were given a choice – denounce your faith or die. The faith of the people was strong and they remained steadfast. The commander closed the church. He chose twenty-five people, lined them up and ordered them to renounce Jesus Christ or die. The people, all twenty-five of them, refused to deny their Lord. They were shot and killed. The next day fifty people were chosen. When all refused to give up their faith, they were shot and killed. On the third day seventy-five were chosen, Anne Marie among them. They, too, were shot and killed – all except Anne Marie. The bullet grazed her head and she began to bleed. One of the soldiers asked the commander if he should kill her. The commander said, "Let her go." Do you think that God had something to do with that decision?

Anne Marie went on to continue her studies. While they were in the Lecture Hall a band of soldiers entered and the students were ordered to get out. They were taken by truck to Auschwitz. Anne Marie thought that she was surely going to die. She started to pray. She and her friend, Christina, along with the others were stripped naked. Everything was taken from them. Those who had gold fillings in their teeth had them knocked out. They were humiliated and forced to march in front of men. Anne Marie had a Rosary that she always wore around her neck. This Rosary was very special to her. It had been given to her by her father when she received her first Holy Communion. He told her to always keep it with her. For some strange reason no one asked her to remove the Rosary which was in plain sight. Was God at work here? Christina said that God had made their eyes blind so that they did not see the Rosary.

Anne Marie and Christina were then sent to be trained as nurses. They were shipped to Warsaw, Poland and put in a military hospital to tend to the wounded soldiers. Not long after that they were sent to the Russian front. There was an unbelievable amount of carnage on the battlefield. At one point Anne Marie was completely exhausted after spending seventy-five hours at the operating table with no rest and no food. She simply could not take any more so she ran away. Anne Marie went into a foxhole. The carnage was horrible. She wanted to die. The words of Jesus came to her, "I am with you. I never leave you."

Suddenly she heard a cry, "Help me. Somebody help me." She was so exhausted she could do nothing. She just lay there. Again, the words came, "Not by your strength, but by My grace." Once more she heard, "Help me." She realized that it was a Russian soldier. She thought, "He is my enemy." She could not help *him*. She would not help him. A gentle voice said, "Love one another as I have loved you." She said, "How can I love him? He is my enemy." Then a strange peace came over her heart as she again heard, "Please someone help me."

Anne Marie said, "All right God. Show me where he is." She found him and immediately she knew that he was going to die as he was mortally wounded. He was in great anguish and knew also that he wasn't long for this world. He managed to get the words out, "Do you know beads – with a cross and a man? I don't know His name." When he was a young boy, his grandmother used to pray with him with the beads. Anne Marie took the Rosary from her neck and showed it to the soldier. He asked her to, "Speak to Him for me. Make the words." Anne Marie baptized him with his own blood and some water from the foxhole. He died in her arms. She said, "Oh my God, You saved the Rosary for him. All along You knew about this child of Yours."[22]

That young soldier went to Christ because his old grandmother who knew Christ prayed for him. He died with the Rosary in his blood-stained hands. Anne Marie left her Rosary with him. She knew that it was where it was meant to be. She came away from this heart-wrenching experience with a much deeper realization that we are all brothers and sisters in Christ – not enemies. Did God's plan work? How many other plans for the salvation of souls does our merciful and loving God have? My guess is that the count is innumerable. Does He have a plan for you? You better believe it!

---

[22] *To Hell And Back, Divine Love and the Cross,* Anne Marie Schmidt, CD, Lighthouse Catholic Media, 2012

When Good Things Happen to Bad People

<u>Officer Jesse Romero</u> of the Los Angeles Sheriff's Department, now retired, tells of his experiences with "bad" kids. On one particular instance while he was on patrol, he caught one young sixteen-year old who was supposed to be in school. Instead he was out on the streets selling marijuana for the purpose of joining a gang. Officer Romero knew this kid and his family. I'll call him Jose. When the handcuffs went on Jose for the purpose of arresting him, he began to plead with Officer Romero. It seems that Jose was out on probation and now he was in violation. This meant that he would go back to jail. Officer Romero decided to make a deal with him. He told Jose that he would take him to meet his best friend and this best friend must become "your" best friend. "I know where you live and if you don't become his best friend, I will come and get you and take you to jail." Reluctantly Jose agreed.

Officer Romero took Jose to Our Lady of Guadalupe Church. This is a beautiful old church with many beautiful statues of saints, of Jesus and Mary. Jose's grandmother had told him about Jesus. He didn't pay much attention to her at the time. Jose was still in handcuffs when they arrived at the church. Inside the church Officer Romero took off the handcuffs and said, "Don't you run away. Get down on your knees." Jesus in the Blessed Sacrament was exposed in a Monstrance for Eucharistic Adoration. Catholics believe that the Sacred Host, the Holy Eucharist, a piece of bread once it is consecrated by the priest becomes the Body of Jesus Christ. This has been proven to be true through many Eucharistic miracles. We will cover this later on in this book.

Now back to Officer Romero and Jose. Jose was on his knees. Officer Romero said, "Now repeat after me. For the sake of His sorrowful passion have mercy on us and on the whole world." He was praying the words of the Chaplet of Divine Mercy. As Jose kept repeating the words, he began crying. Officer Romero asked him, "Why are you crying?" Jose replied, "I have never felt so much love in my entire life. I don't ever want to leave this place."

This kid, Jose, who never went to church, whose parents did not attend church, melted before Jesus in the Blessed Sacrament. Officer Romero took him to school. He did not join the gang that was trying to recruit him. Instead Jose joined the Confirmation class with Officer Romero becoming his sponsor. He graduated from high school, went on to college and became a successful businessman. He married and had two beautiful children.

Jose tells people that if he had not been caught by Officer Romero at the age of sixteen, he would have been in prison like his father and his brother.[23] Is there any other god who can reach into one's heart and effect an immediate and permanent change? There is only one God Who can do that – Yahweh, the Creator, Jesus Lord and Master of the Universe, along with the power of the Holy Spirit. How awesome it that!

Where will you go?

The people who are good go to heaven. What about those who are good most of the time, but still have some sins on their soul when they die? No one is perfect. We all have our little and sometimes big sins. We repent; then, because of our human weakness, find ourselves doing the same things over and over again. Yes, Jesus died and paid the price for our sins so that we could have the chance to go to heaven. However, we know in our hearts that we are not worthy of heaven, and yet, we are not so wicked as to deserve hell for *all eternity*. Is there a middle ground? Let's see.

23　*Life Changing Stories of the Eucharist,* Jesse Romero, CD, Lighthouse Catholic Media, 2012

A sense of justice demands that we be held accountable for our actions, that we make amends for the wrongs we have done. If we die still with some stain of sin on our soul, how can we be admitted into heaven which is a place of all purity and holiness? How can we stand before an all Holy God with a stained garment so to speak? We need to be pure and holy before being admitted to His holy abode. Does that make sense to you? So then, where do we go in the meantime until we are cleansed so that we can then be admitted into heaven? Purgatory? Some Christian denominations believe that there is no purgatory. Catholic Christians believe that there is indeed a purgatory. What is the truth?

What does the Bible say?

When Jesus was dying on the cross, we read "One of the criminals hanging in crucifixion blasphemed Him: 'Aren't You the Messiah? Then save Yourself and us.' But the other one rebuked him: 'Have you no fear of God, seeing you are under the same sentence? We deserve it, after all. We are only paying the price for what we have done, but this Man has done nothing wrong.' He then said, 'Jesus, remember me when You enter into Your reign.' And Jesus replied, 'I assure you, this day you will be with Me in paradise.'" (Luke 23: 39-43)

Some people will interpret this passage to mean that because Jesus died and paid the price for our sins, we will go straight to heaven if we believe even though we still have some stains of sin on our soul. Does this seem reasonable? Could it be that Jesus assured the "Good Thief" that *he* would go straight to heaven because he repented of his sins, and he was making restitution for them as he hung on the cross? Remember that crucifixion was the most barbarous form of execution that ever existed – first being scourged so as to weaken the person, then being nailed to a cross and to have the blood slowly ooze from one's body, excruciating physical pain, unable to move or change one's position, the need to push up on one's feet in order to breathe and that with great difficulty, exhaustion – all this, not to mention the humiliation of dying as a criminal. And finally, his legs were broken. "Accordingly, the soldiers came and broke the legs of the men crucified with Jesus, first of the one, then of the other." (John 19:32) Imagine going through all this pain and suffering. Don't you think that this man paid for all his sins and was indeed ready to go straight to heaven?

Now let's go back to our question – is there a Purgatory? The Bible says, "it is a holy and wholesome thought to pray for the dead that *they may be loosed from their sins.* What do you think is the correct interpretation of this passage? If they are in heaven, wouldn't they already be loosed from their sins? They would no longer need our prayers.

God is all holy and nothing defiled can stand in His holy presence. ". . .but nothing profane shall enter it, nor anyone who is a liar or has done a detestable act. Only those shall enter whose names are inscribed in the book of the living kept by the Lamb." (Revelation 21:27) When we die and God asks us, "What have you done with your life?" How will we answer? We then see a complete review of our entire life. "The Father has given over to Him power to pass judgment because He is Son of Man." (John 5:27) Jesus is the Just Judge as He well deserves to be because He gave totally of Himself unto death to pay the price for our sins. But it seems that He is not so much being judgmental as that we are judging ourselves. The light of truth shines in us, and we convict ourselves of the wrongs we have done – no rationalizations, no excuses, no lying to ourselves any more and, of course, there is no lying to God because He *knows all.* If we have committed great wrongs and are unrepentant, we banish ourselves to hell because we *know* that is what we deserve. If we were exemplary in our behavior, we *know* it and our destiny is heaven because we love God above all else so much that we wish to be with Him forever.

Someone like St. Mother Teresa of Calcutta, India would probably fill the bill to go straight to heaven. Her entire life was devoted to the service and love of God through caring for the poor, sick, and dying people of Calcutta regardless of how dirty they were, or their religious beliefs. She questioned no one who came to her but tended to his/her needs giving loving care in heroic measure. Very few of us can honestly say that we have done likewise and have no stain of sin left in us when we die.

Are there any other Bible references to Purgatory?

Since we must be accountable for the wrongs we have done, we must make restitution for them. In the Bible, the book of Maccabees, we read that we should pray for the dead *that they may be loosed from their sins.* Why do they need to be loosed from their sins? Where are they if not in heaven?

". . .but nothing profane shall enter into it, nor anyone who is a liar or has done a detestable act." (Revelation 21:27) If nothing profane can enter into God's presence in heaven, then how can a person who still has some stain of sin on his/her soul go to heaven?

Let's check the Bible again. "But the souls of the just are in the hand of God, and no torment shall touch them. . .Chastised a little, they shall be greatly blessed, because God tried them and found them worthy of Himself." (Wisdom 3:1,5) *Chastised a little, they shall be greatly blessed.* Where will they be chastised; how will they be chastised? Purgatory? That makes sense. Don't you think so?

Some people believe that in some cases we have our purgatory right here on earth. Is that true? That may very well be. If you look around, you will see people with all kinds of suffering. Is it because of their sins? Only God can answer that. There are people in hospitals, nursing homes, prisons, intolerable living and working conditions. There are people who suffer from abuse, from neglect, from oppression. Is it because of their sins? I don't know. Could this be their purgatory? Possibly? Only God knows for sure.

What is Purgatory like?

OK, so we've caught a glimpse of heaven. Now, what is Purgatory like? Can anyone tell us; does anyone really know?

In Purgatory – "desire with the absolute certainty of being satisfied is both joy and pain. . .The Holy Souls are happy because by God's grace and their own free will they have secured the certainty of seeing and enjoying Him, whom they supremely love. They are sad because through their own fault they are deprived (temporarily) of the blissful vision of His glory. Purgatory, not unlike heaven, is a place of rest. All the petty anxieties of life have gone. All of the unruly cravings and longings are gone. . .we know that we are saved. Yet, Purgatory is a place of untold sorrow. . .We commonly speak of a burning desire. Even on earth an unsatisfied desire may become an acute mental pain, a consuming anguish greater than any torture by physical hurt."[24] The loss of a loved one, the loss of honor or goods, disgrace, humiliation, shame, rejection by a loved one – these things can hurt more than any physical pain.

The most acute pain in purgatory is being deprived of seeing God. Our longing to be with Him is most intense. Because of their great desire to be with God, the Holy Souls in purgatory suffer intolerably. Is there fire in purgatory? Blessed Anne Catherine Emmerich, an Augustinian nun who bore the stigmata (wounds of Christ) saw many

---

24   *Purgatory and Heaven*, J.P. Arendzen, D.D., pp. 19-21

visions including that of purgatory. She describes it as a place of great suffering; however, she does not mention any fire.

St. Faustina Kowalska wrote in her diary on page 20 regarding purgatory, "I was in a place full of fire in which there was a great crowd of suffering souls. . .I asked these souls what their greatest suffering was. They answered me in one voice that their greatest torment was longing for God. . .I heard an inner voice which said 'My mercy does not want this, but justice demands it'. . .I did not know that even the smallest transgressions will have to be accounted for."

What else did I learn?

In my readings I came across the account of a poor soul in purgatory named Rachel who appeared as an old woman with charred clothing smelling of smoke. She explained that purgatory should not be feared, but seen as a grace. It is a place or reparation for sins that are forgiven but not atoned for, a place where the soul is perfected in preparation for entrance into eternal joy. It is also a place of separation from God – the greatest suffering of all. Purgatory does indeed exist and disbelief does not allow one to avoid it and can be a reason for a longer stay.

Rachel went on to explain that free will choices affect a person's eternity. Many people are in purgatory because they tried to please themselves or others rather than God. There are different levels in purgatory as there are in heaven and hell, depending on one's sins. For example, a person who has committed murder, then repented will have much greater suffering than a person who was guilty of stealing small items from a department store.

Basically there are three forms of suffering in purgatory. The first is physical. It is the lowest region and can be as intense as the fires of hell. There is extreme desolation and loneliness. The second level is not so much physical as emotional abandonment. The third level closest to heaven is where the only suffering is the desire to be with God. In all levels, the desire to be with God is very intense. Each soul's experience is different according to his/her life choices. Some suffer intense fire, others loneliness, still others a burning tongue for lying, etc. Just as crosses and graces are individual to each soul, so is the purgatory experience.

Is there help?

Is there anything that can be done by us here on earth to help the Holy Souls in their suffering? Yes, we can pray for them as mentioned in Maccabees that they may be loosed from their sins, have Masses offered for them, give alms to the needy in their behalf, make sacrifices for them and self-denials. This will render some relief to them. Rachel also explained that souls are unaware of the passage of time or how long they will be there. When prayers or sacrifices are offered up for them, they are somewhat relieved and are moved closer to heaven, most rapidly by the Holy Mass offered for them, and next the Rosary. However, every prayer, every sacrifice, no matter how small is welcomed. The souls in purgatory, even though they suffer much, have a deep profound peace because they know that they are saved and will eventually be with God. Purgatory is indeed a grace from and all-merciful God.[25]

Many people don't pray for their family members and friends because they believe that they are in heaven. This is a mistake not to pray for them. They may very well be in heaven, but perhaps not. We really don't know. If they are in purgatory, then our prayers can help them to get to heaven sooner. They will suffer until their debt is paid so to speak or they are purged of all stain of sin. If they are already in

---

25   Holy Love Messages, October 22-29, 2010, Holy Love Ministries, Maranatha Spring and Shrine, Elyria, Ohio

heaven, our prayers are not wasted. They will be applied to someone else who perhaps has no one to pray for him/her. No prayer is ever wasted. Can the Holy Souls help those of us still on earth? Yes, they can pray for us and intercede for individual gifts and graces that we wish to receive from God. This is called the Communion of Saints.

Isn't God wonderful? Think of it. Even though His justice as well as our own sense of justice demands that we are accountable and make restitution for our actions, He gives us a way out. Our sins may be most grievous; we may deserve to spend our eternity in hell, and we know it. Still, His mercy is far greater than our sins, and He is always willing to give us another chance, to take us back even though we do not deserve it. We should never hesitate to return to God because we think that our sins are too great or too many. When we come back and repent of all our sins, however, we know that we do not deserve heaven after committing all those sins. But because of His great love and goodness, God has created Purgatory whereby we can make amends and eventually get to heaven where we will be eternally happy. Because of God's incomprehensible mercy, we will be able to give Him the honor, glory, love, and praise that He rightly deserves forever. FANTASTIC! Is there anyone who can even come close to the greatness of our God?!!

By the way, Rachel did finally get to heaven. She appeared as a beautiful young woman radiant with joy, all dressed exquisitely in white. She stated, "Please allow me to thank the people who prayed for me into heaven. I was in purgatory for many years for the sin of not examining the errors in my own heart, and not trying to correct them. There are thousands, even millions, still imprisoned there for the same reason."

The Bad: How Bad Are We?

If you make it a habit to pray for the souls in purgatory and help them to get to heaven sooner, think of how many will pray for you when your turn comes. Now that's what I call a win-win situation. Don't you agree?

Chapter 3

The Ugly: Can They Be Saved?

Who are they?

These are the people who commit horrific crimes against other people. They are the embezzlers, those who steal large sums of money from charitable organizations, financial institutions, who make themselves rich by defrauding many people. These are the violent people who break into other people's homes to steal and possibly physically harm anyone who gets in their way. Drug dealers destroy lives by pushing young people into addiction. Human traffickers enslave people. All this for the love of money. Then there are the rapists and murderers. How can any of these people eventually get into heaven? Let's take some examples.

<u>Bernie Madoff</u> – Remember him? He was a wealthy man, smart, a genius to some. So why did Bernie Madoff concoct an elaborate Ponzi scheme that bilked thousands of clients, including business leaders, celebrities, charities, even some of his own relatives and his defense attorney (he fooled his lawyer?) out of $65 billion? What is a Ponzi scheme anyway? Named after Charles Ponzi, the first criminal to use it, a Ponzi scheme takes in people's money to be invested for them at a

high rate of interest, or so they are told. The person who manages the money, in this case Bernie Madoff, uses the money collected from new investors to cover the money owed to old investors who want their money paid to them. It works quite well until too many people want their money and the whole scam collapses. The perpetrator is then indicted for fraud. Was Bernie's method illegal? You bet it was. On March 12, 2009, Madoff pled guilty to eleven felonies and admitted to the largest investor fraud ever committed by an individual.

On June 29, 2009, a federal judge, U.S. District Judge Denny Chin rejected Madoff's plea for leniency in the multi-billion dollar fraud case. He was given the maximum penalty for each of the eleven felonies bringing his prison term to a grand total of 150 years, a term comparable to those only given to the most violent criminals, terrorists, and traitors. Bernie will probably die in prison since there is no parole in federal prisons. At 71 years old, he would have to live to be 221 years of age in order to fulfill his prison time. Judge Chin stated, "Here, the message must be sent that Mr. Madoff's crimes were extraordinarily evil and that this kind of irresponsible manipulation of the system is not merely a bloodless financial crime that takes place on paper, but is instead. . .one that takes a staggering human toll."[26]

Why did Judge Chin give such a harsh sentence? Obviously, he took into consideration the fact that the massive Ponzi scheme that Madoff concocted financially destroyed thousands of investors. What about all the victims? Bernie Madoff's victims included ordinary citizens to the Hollywood elites. He stole from the rich; he stole from the average; he stole from charitable organizations. The sad part is that some of these people were depending on their investment money for their retirement years, and now it is gone. Some of the charities had to

---

26   Hays, Tom and Larry Neumeister, "Madoff gets maximum," AP, Hazleton Standard-Speaker, June 30, 2009, p. A1

close their doors because their investments are gone. And what other burdens have been put on people or businesses because of his fraudulent behavior? Bernie Madoff gave a statement, "I cannot offer you an excuse for my behavior. How do you excuse betraying thousands of investors who entrusted me with their life savings? How do you excuse deceiving 200 employees who spent most of their working life with me? How do you excuse lying to a brother and two sons who spent their entire lives helping me to build a successful business? How do you excuse lying to a wife who stood by me for 50 years?" Putting him in jail is not going to fix all the problems he caused. At best, it will give some the satisfaction of knowing that he is paying for his crime.

And what about his family? Are they victims, too? They have to bear the scandal and disgrace. Their assets have been frozen, most of which are being liquidated and given to the investors although it will not nearly satisfy the amount that was defrauded from them. How much will the family have to give up to make restitution for these crimes? At least $1 billion in recovered assets will be returned to the investors and perhaps a lot more.

It was the worst investment fraud in American history. Could there possibly be any more heartache to this story? Unfortunately, there is. The mounting pressures of the investigation, the family disgrace, the unrelenting press coverage, false accusations and innuendo, and investor lawsuits proved to be too much for Bernie's son, Mark. The 46-year old took his own life by hanging. He emailed his wife, told her he loved her, and that someone should check on their two-year old son who was sleeping in a room nearby. He left no suicide note. It was he and his brother, Andrew, who notified the authorities that their father had confessed his crime to them. Neither had spoken to their father since his arrest on December 11, 2008.

What a sad, heartbreaking state of affairs. All this, and why? Money. How much pain has been caused; how many lives have been adversely affected or destroyed? All for money – a temporary commodity. You can't take it with you when you are called into the next world by the Eternal Lord.

Is it over for Bernie now that he has been sentenced? Not by a long shot! He will have to carry the burden of knowing that his actions caused his son to take his own life. He still has to face the Eternal Judge. Then what? Will Bernie be forgiven? By whom? There are probably many people who will never forgive him especially if they lost their life savings. That's understandable. What about the innocent family members and workers who were clueless as to his activities? How are they coping with all this? Will God forgive him? Well, that depends on Bernie himself. What does he believe? Will he truly repent of his sins? God will *always* forgive the truly repentant sinner.

<u>Ted Bundy</u> – It was the middle of the night in 1978 in Tallahassee, Florida when Father Kerr got a call from the Police to quickly come to the sorority house. In response to this emergency call, Father Kerr rushed to the scene where he found young female victims of the serial killer Ted Bundy dead or dying. All but one of the girls had been attacked. After attending to the needs of the dying, Father Kerr was asked to talk to the girl who survived untouched by Ted Bundy in his brutal attack on the others. The terrified girl refused to talk to anyone but a priest. The Police wanted to know how she survived because Ted Bundy had stopped right inside her door, dropped his weapon, and left without touching her. When she spoke to Father Kerr, she told him that, before going off to college, her mother made her promise to say the Rosary every night for her protection even if she fell asleep before finishing the Rosary. That night when Ted Bundy came into

The Ugly: Can They Be Saved?

her room with the intention of murder on his mind, the Rosary beads were in her hand.

Some years later Ted Bundy would tell the now Monsignor Kerr who became his spiritual advisor in prison, that when he entered that girl's room, he just couldn't go on. It was like a strong force was preventing him from going any further with his murderous rampage. So he dropped his weapon and fled.

On January 24, 1989, the day before Ted's execution was scheduled, James C. Dobson, psychologist, was granted permission to interview the infamous serial killer responsible for the brutal murders of as many as fifty young girls and women. Asked if his was a childhood in which he was abused physically, sexually, or emotionally, Ted answered, "No." He explained that he grew up in a "wonderful home with two loving parents as one of five brothers and sisters." They attended church regularly. "It was a fine Christian home." What went wrong in Ted's life? Ted went on to explain that as a young boy of 12 or 13, he became involved in pornography which gradually led to an addiction and eventually to fantasies and to murder.

Ted Bundy was deeply remorseful for all the pain and sorrow caused to the victims and their families. He accepted the forgiveness of Jesus Christ and said that he drew strength from Jesus as he approached his final hour. Ted Bundy was executed at 7:15 a.m. the day after this interview.

Did Ted Bundy deserve to go to hell for all those horrible murders? Yes, he did deserve to go to hell. He knew what he was doing; he knew that it was wrong; he knew he was responsible for his actions. At that point Satan probably believed that Ted Bundy belonged to him, and Satan was probably right. But Ted's family members and others must have been praying for him. During all those years in prison he must have relived all that horror many times over because he was remorseful and begged God's forgiveness. In all likelihood, God in His mercy forgave Ted because God is love and does not want the destruction of any of His children. By God's grace Ted Bundy was able to seek forgiveness and to save his soul. Even if he spends a very long time in purgatory paying for his sins, he will eventually get to heaven. That is far better than going to hell for all eternity. What do you think about that? How great is our God!

<u>Karla Faye Tucker</u> – born and raised in Houston, Texas, was the daughter of a longshoreman on the Gulf of Mexico. He was in a very troubled marriage that ended in divorce when Karla was ten years old. At this time Karla learned that she had been the result of an extramarital affair. By the age of twelve she was into drugs and sex. At fourteen she dropped out of school and followed her mother into prostitution. She was married at sixteen for a very short time and in her early twenties began hanging out with bikers. She met Shawn Dean and her husband, Jerry Dean, and in 1981 met Danny Garrett.

In June 1983 Shawn and Jerry broke up as Jerry had a new girlfriend, Debbie Thornton. On June 11, Tucker and Garrett got high on drugs along with James Liebrant. They decided to steal Jerry's motorcycle. Jerry confronted them in the process of the burglary in his home at which time Garrett began to strike him numerous times with a hammer. Debbie Thornton, hiding under the covers was discovered by Tucker who then hacked her to death with a pickaxe. The next morning, the landlord discovered the bodies. Investigation led to the arrests of Tucker and Garrett. In September 1983, Tucker and Garrett were indicted and tried separately for murder. Tucker pleaded not guilty and was jailed awaiting trial. The prison ministry offered her a Bible, and she read it in her jail cell. She found herself on her knees asking God's forgiveness. In the spring of 1984, she confessed

The Ugly: Can They Be Saved?

to the murders and implicated Garrett. They were both convicted and later sentenced to death in 1984. Tucker became a Christian in 1985.

Karla Faye Tucker was visited by many celebrities including Sister Helen Prejean, author of *Dead Man Walking*, about whom a movie was made of the same name starring Susan Sarandon as Sister Helen. There was an application to the Texas Board of Pardons and Parole in an attempt for clemency. Tucker requested that her life be spared on the basis that she was under the influence of drugs at the time of the murders. Her plea drew support from many who appealed to the State of Texas on her behalf. Among those were Waly Bacre Ndiaye, the United Nations commissioner on summary and arbitrary executions; the World Council of Churches, Pope John Paul II; Italian Prime Minister Romano Prodi; the Speaker of the U.S. House of Representatives Newt Gingrich; Rev. Pat Robertson, televangelist; and Ron Carlson, the brother of Tucker's murder victim, Debbie Thornton. All this, however, was to no avail, and on February 2, 1998, expressing her sorrow to the Thornton and Dean families, and thanking everyone for being so good to her, Karla Faye Tucker was executed by lethal injection.[27]

Did Karla deserve to go to hell? Some say yes. Others would take into consideration that she was under the influence of drugs at the time. However, she was sincerely remorseful and asked forgiveness from God and from the families of the victims. God does not desire the destruction of any of His children. God's mercy is greater than any sin. God will forgive any sin if a person is truly sorry.

St. Rita of Cascia (1381-1457) – was married at the age of twelve at the insistence of her aged parents who wanted to insure that she would be protected and not become an orphan. Rita married Paolo Mancini a rich quick-tempered, immoral man who had many enemies

---

27   *Karla Faye Tucker*, Wikipedia

When Good Things Happen to Bad People

in the region of Cascia in Italy. Rita endured his insults, physical abuse, and infidelities for many years including a family feud between the Mancini and Chiqui families. A vendetta existed between the families whereby one murdered family member was avenged by murdering a member of the other family.

Rita and Paolo had two sons. Through humility, kindness, and patience, Rita was able to convert her husband in renouncing the family feud. The feud intensified and Paolo's allies betrayed him. He was violently stabbed to death by Guido Chiqui, a member of the other feuding family. Rita publicly forgave her husband's murderers at his funeral. Paolo's brother, Bernardo, continued the feud and tried to convince Rita's two sons to seek revenge through murder. He convinced the two young boys to leave their mother and to live with him at the Mancini ancestral home. He taught them that they should avenge their father's murder. Rita, fearing that they would lose their souls, petitioned God to take them rather than for them to commit murder. Her sons died of dysentery a year later with the consolations of the Church.

After the death of her husband and sons, Rita desired to enter the monastery of Saint Mary Magdalene in Cascia but was refused. The nuns were afraid of being associated with her due to the continuing family feud and her husband's violent death. When she persisted, she was told that she could enter on the condition that she must seek reconciliation between the two families and bring peace. At that time the bubonic plague was rampant in Italy and had infected Bernardo Mancini. Rita was able to bring both families together in reconciliation and peace – no more murders. The conflicts were resolved and Rita, at the age of thirty-six, was allowed to enter the monastery.

St. Rita died at the age of seventy-six. Her body has remained incorrupt for centuries to this day. She was canonized by Pope

Leo XIII on May 24, 1900 and was bestowed the title *Patroness of Impossible Causes*. She is known as the patroness of abused women and heartbroken women.

God in His great mercy brought salvation to Rita's husband, their sons, his brother Bernardo, along with some other members of the feuding families through the prayers, kindness, and patience of Rita. God always finds a way to bring salvation to His children who are open to it. It is mostly done through other loving people. What a wonderful way to promote His love among brothers and sisters.

What does Dr. Bernard Nathanson have to say?

"I am personally responsible for 75,000 abortions. . .I was one of the founders of the National Association for the Repeal of the Abortion Laws (NARAL) in the U.S. in 1968. . .most Americans were against permissive abortion. Yet within five years we had convinced the U.S. Supreme Court to issue the decision which legalized abortion throughout America in 1973 and produced virtual abortion on demand up to birth."[28]

In his confession Dr. Nathanson explains how they lied to the media stating that the majority of Americans wanted legalized abortion. They fabricated results of fictional polls. The number of women having illegal abortions was 200-250 annually. They inflated that figure to 10,000 and continued to push lies until the public bought it. Dr. Nathanson explained that they vilified the Catholic Church for being "socially backward' and the Catholic hierarchy for opposing abortion. Then they suppressed all scientific evidence that life begins at conception.

---

28   Confession of An EX-Abortionist, by Dr. Bernard Nathanson, M.D.

What made him change his mind? Foetology which is the study of the foetus (fetus) in the womb. "Foetology makes it undeniably evident that life begins at conception. . ." So why do American doctors who know this continue to perform abortions? "Simple arithmetic at $300 a time, 1.55 million abortions means an industry generating $500,000,000 annually, (of course, these figures are much higher today) most of which goes into the pocket of the physician doing the abortion. . .an impermissible act of deadly violence. As a scientist I know, not believe, that life begins at conception." You can read his full confession on the Internet.

Dr. Nathanson had been involved in abortion for thirty years. After years involving much anguish of heart, three failed marriages, and thoughts of suicide, he began reading and searching for answers to assuage his battered conscience. God Who is loving and merciful, seeing his remorseful anguished heart, pursued him as He pursues each and every one of us who stray away from Him. Dr. Nathanson became acquainted with Father John McCloskey, a Catholic priest. Father McCloskey helped Dr. Nathanson to understand a loving and forgiving God, Jesus Christ His Son, and the sacrament of Baptism which washed away all sin and guilt, enabling him to become a new man. Dr. Nathanson converted to Catholicism and was baptized in 1996. The prayers of thousands of pro-life Christians of all denominations who had prayed for years had been answered.[29] The complete article can be found on the Internet.

<u>Dr. George Tiller</u> became known as "Tiller the baby killer." He performed many late-term abortions using the horrible partial-birth abortion method. Antiabortion/pro-life groups claimed he was performing late-term abortions for relatively minor fetal abnormalities. Dr. Tiller himself acknowledged performing abortions on healthy

---

29 "Bernard Nathanson's Conversion," by Julia Duin

babies. His patients included girls as young as ten, rape victims, alcoholics, drug addicts, women who were depressed/suicidal, as well as anyone who wanted an abortion. In the 1990's he bought a second clinic and tried to acquire a third clinic. Over the years he was responsible for some 60,000 abortions. Why? Money – at $5,000 and more recently $6,000 for each abortion, he became a multimillionaire. Was it worth it? Where is he now? In 1991 anti-abortion groups launched a massive protest against his clinic known as Operation Rescue. It lasted more than six weeks and resulted in about 2800 arrests. Still, Dr. Tiller continued his gruesome profession.

In 1993, Dr. Tiller was shot in both arms outside his clinic. It became necessary for him to fortify his clinic, and he was forced to hire a bodyguard.[30] On Sunday, May 31, 2009, Dr. George Tiller was shot and killed at his church, the Reformation Lutheran Church in Wichita, Kansas. Troy Newman, president of Operation Rescue denounced this deadly act of violence and stated that for years they have worked through peaceful, legal means, and proper channels to see him brought to justice.

The National Right to Life Committee (NRLC), the nation's largest pro-life organization condemned the killing of Dr. Tiller stating that the NRLC "unequivocally condemns any such acts of violence regardless of motivation. The pro-life movement works to protect life. The unlawful use of violence is directly contrary to that goal. . .NRLC's sole purpose is to protect innocent human life."[31]

Dr. Alveda King, Pastoral Associate of Priests for Life, and the niece of Dr. Martin Luther King, Jr., stated that the killing of late-term abortionist, Dr. George Tiller, brings tremendous sorrow. She had

---

30   "Profile: George Tiller," BBC News/America
31   "The Wrong Release," Kathryn Jean Lopez, *The Corner, National Review*

visited his clinic in 2007 in the hope of bringing about his repentance. Dr. King said, "I am deeply sorry that his life was taken before that could happen."[32]

On June 9, 2009, Shepard Smith on FOX News reported that the family of Dr. George Tiller announced that the abortion clinic would be permanently closed. This is a bitter-sweet victory for pro-life advocates – bitter because of the violent, senseless murder of Dr. Tiller; sweet because of the knowledge that with the closing of the clinic, the lives of precious babies would be saved.

Was Dr. Tiller prepared to meet his Maker? Only God knows for sure. All we know is that he was given plenty of warnings and opportunities to turn away from the horrific evil of performing abortions. Good Christian people prayed for him, tried to reach him, protested against the evil. Did he listen? Did he feel any remorse for all the babies destroyed by his hands? Was there *any* mercy in his soul for all the little angels made in the image and likeness of God who died in excruciating pain? Did God, our Heavenly Father, weep bitterly every time another baby, member of His family, was destroyed? All we can do now is pray for God's mercy and that all those connected with this holocaust-type clinic will come to realize the horror of what they are doing and repent of this grave sin before it is too late for them, also.

Dr. Kermit B. Gosnell owned and operated a "front alley" abortion clinic. What is that? In an effort to eliminate so-called back alley abortions in environments lacking minimal medical standards, abortion was made legal to protect and aid women, especially poor women who were "going to get an abortion anyway." While there is some truth that legal abortions have diminished the inflated incidences of back alley abortions in America, there is an even greater danger to

---

[32] "Dr. Alveda King – Sorrow that Dr. Tiller Didn't Live to Repent," Christian Newswire

The Ugly: Can They Be Saved?

women, especially poor women, of the "front alley" abortions which take place in *legal* abortion mills. They are open to the public and have the appearances of legitimate businesses and are protected by the government since abortion is legal *under the law*. Some of these clinics commit the most horrible acts.

The Women's Medical Society, a clinic in West Philadelphia, Pennsylvania, operated by Kermit B. Gosnell, M.D., was Gosnell's House of Horrors. "According to the district attorney's report, Gosnell staffed his unsanitary clinic with unlicensed personnel, let them practice medicine on unsuspecting patients without supervision, and directed them to drug patients heavily in his absence. In addition, he regularly performed abortions beyond the 24-week legal limit. Hence, when viable babies were born, Gosnell killed them by plunging scissors where the head joins the spinal cord. He also taught his staff to do the same."[33] Dr. Gosnell and nine of his staff employees were arrested for a mother's accidental death due to an overdose of drugs, the murder of seven viable infants, and violations of illegal medical practices. While in prison, Dr. Gosnell and his employees still have the opportunity to seek forgiveness and to be reconciled to God. But will they do so?

Other houses of horror have been found. For example, the Texas Medical Board received complaints about the medical practices of twelve Texas abortion providers. The nature of abortion is a tragic denial of our human dignity made in the image and likeness of God. It leads to that which is inhuman. Abortion at any stage from conception on is murder of an innocent human being. How does God view the destruction of even one of His children? In our country and

---

[33] *Front Alley Abortions*, John Horvat II, Crusade Magazine, July/August 2011, p. 5

around the world, the slaughter of the innocents, human sacrifice, must be the most abhorrent to an all-holy God Who is all love.

On June 24, 2022, the Supreme Court ruled in Dobbs v. Jackson Women's Health Organization – a case involving a challenge to a Mississippi ban on abortion at 15 weeks of pregnancy. The ruling overturned Roe v. Wade ending the constitutional right to abortion in the United States. "In Roe v. Wade, the Supreme Court decided that the right to privacy implied in the 14th Amendment protected abortion as a fundamental right. However, the government retained the power to regulate or restrict abortion access depending on the stage of pregnancy."[34] In the June 24, 2022 ruling, the Supreme Court determined that women *do not have a Constitutional right* to choose to terminate their pregnancies and overturned the 50-year precedent established in Roe v. Wade.

What does this mean? The legal authority to decide on the abortion issue now reverts back to the states. Each state has the authority to determine whether abortion will be legal in that state, what kinds of restrictions will be enforced, or whether abortion will be completely banned. Some states are keeping abortion legal, some are imposing more strict restrictions, and some states are working to ban abortion completely. While the battle rages on regarding women's rights, one factor is somewhat overlooked – the rights of the baby. Our Constitution does not mention any right to abortion. It does, however, mention the right of every person to life, liberty, and the pursuit of happiness. The baby is guaranteed the right to life by our Constitution.

(See Appendix C – The Abortion Issue)

---

34   Brennan Center for Justice

The Ugly: Can They Be Saved?

Now back to other houses of horror that have been found. The Texas Medical Board received complaints about the medical practices of twelve Texas abortion providers. The nature of abortion is a tragic denial of our human dignity made in the image and likeness of God. It leads to that which is inhuman. Abortion at any stage from conception on is murder of an innocent human being. How does God view the destruction of even one of His children? In our country and around the world, the slaughter of the innocents, human sacrifice, must be the most abhorrent to an all-holy God Who is all love. How will those who do not abandon this evil practice and seek forgiveness end up? Hell, perhaps?

Hell – what is it like?

Does hell really exist? How can a loving God allow it? If so, what is it like? Satan is very clever. The more he can convince people that there is no hell, the easier it is to get people to give in to temptation, and as you well know, one sin leads to another until you are hooked. Satan wants your soul, and he will do anything to get you in his clutches.

So how do we know that hell really exists? Check out the Bible. There are at least thirty references in the Old Testament alone. "The Lord Almighty will take revenge on them, in the day of judgment He will visit them. For He will give fire and worms into their flesh, that they may burn, and may feel forever." (Judith 16:17) Jesus says, "The Son of Man will dispatch His angels to collect from his kingdom all who draw others to sin and all evildoers. The angels will hurl them into the fiery furnace where they will wail and grind their teeth." (Matthew 13:41-42)

Jesus also describes the last judgment as the separating of the sheep (those who loved God and neighbor) from the goats (those who did not love God and neighbor). He says, "Depart from Me, you accursed, into the eternal fire prepared for the devil and his angels. ...And these will go off to eternal punishment, but the righteous to eternal life." (Matthew 25:41-46) Jesus is very clear – by the choices we make in this life to disobey God's commandments, we risk eternal punishment after death – *we risk hell.*

We have seen that there are people who have had a wonderful glimpse of heaven and those who have seen purgatory. Are there any who have seen what hell is really like? Is it as frightening as the Old Testament and the New Testament of the Bible tell us? Why would a loving God let some people see this horror? "The dogma of hell stands on the infallible Word of God; but in His mercy, God, to aid our faith, permits at intervals, the truth of hell to be manifested in a sensible manner."[35]

Has anyone seen hell?

Now let's look at some examples of people who have seen what hell is really like. During the canonization process (declaration of the sanctity of a person by the Catholic Church) of St. Francis Jerome (1642-1716) a large number of eye witnesses testified under oath to the following account: St. Francis was preaching about Hell and the awful chastisement that awaits obstinate sinners. A brazen prostitute tried to silence his teachings by shouts and noise. St. Francis called out to her, "Beware, my daughter, of resisting grace; before eight days God will punish you." She did not take the heed and only became more boisterous. Eight days later she suddenly died. St. Francis said, "Dead! Well, let her tell us now what she has gained by laughing at Hell. Let us ask her." Followed by an immense crowd, he went up to the death chamber, said a short prayer, then uncovered the face of the corpse and said, "Catherine, tell us where you are now." The

---

35 *Hell*, Fr. F.X. SCHOUPPE, S.J., pp. 5, 6

dead woman lifted her head, opened her eyes, her features assuming an expression of horrible despair, and in a mournful voice said, "In Hell; I am in Hell." Then she fell back into the condition of a corpse.[36] Remember that there was a large number of eye witnesses to this event who testified under oath.

<u>St. Faustina</u>, a Polish nun who was canonized by Pope John Paul II on April 30, 2000, was shown the vision of hell in 1936. In her diary she wrote, "It is a place of great torture. . .the first torture is the loss of God; the second is perpetual remorse of conscience;. . .one's condition will never change;. . .the fire that will penetrate the soul without destroying it – a terrible suffering, a purely spiritual fire;. . .continual darkness and a terrible suffocating smell; the devils and the souls of the damned see each other and all the evil of others and their own; the constant company of Satan; horrible despair, hatred of God, vile words, curses, and blasphemies. These are tortures suffered by all the damned. Also, there are special tortures each soul undergoes of terrible and indescribable sufferings related to the manner in which he (or she) sinned. The sinner will be tortured throughout all eternity in those senses which he (or she) made use of to sin. I am writing this at the command of God, so that no soul may find an excuse by saying there is no hell, or that nobody has ever been there, and so no one can say what is it like. . .that I might tell souls about it and testify to its existence. . .What I have written is but a pale shadow of the things I saw. But I noticed one thing: that most of the souls there are those who disbelieved that there is a hell."[37]

<u>In 1917, the Virgin Mary</u> appeared to three children, Lucia age 10, Francisco age 9, and Jacinta age 7 at Fatima, Portugal. On July 13, 1917 she showed them a vision of hell. They described a sea of fire

---

36 Ibid, p. 56
37 *Devine Mercy in My Soul*, Diary of Sister M. Faustina Kowalska

containing demons and souls in human form in excruciating torment and shrieks and groans of pain and despair. The children screamed and trembled with fear; they were terrified. The Blessed Virgin gave them a special prayer to be said after each mystery of the Rosary: "O my Jesus, forgive us our sins, save us from the fires of hell and lead all souls to heaven, especially those in most need of Your mercy." "Yes, the Blessed Virgin showed Hell to a little girl of seven, with demons in the form of horrible monsters, and the souls of the damned burning in a huge fire! Why would she do such a thing? That vision transformed Jacinta's life: from then on she agreed to suffer so that sinners could convert, and therefore avoid losing their souls forever."[38]

Little Jacinta offered many prayers and sacrifices for poor sinners because she had seen the horrors of hell and didn't want anyone to go there for all eternity. She died just shy of the age of ten. Jacinta and Francisco Marto were both canonized as saints in the Catholic Church by Pope Francis in Fatima, Portugal on May 13, 2017.

<u>George</u> had died at the tender age of 20, barely grown. Nine minutes later he returned to life. This event occurred in December 1943. His book *Return from Tomorrow* relates the experience of what he saw of heaven and hell. Since heaven is already covered, we will concentrate on his vision of hell. He had encountered and been in the presence of Jesus, the Son of God, as a living Light beside him and guiding him.

George explained how loved he felt even when the question was put to him, "What did you do with your life?" He was shown every part of his life up to that point –. "How much have you loved with your life? Have you loved others as I am loving you? Totally? Unconditionally? George found himself not being judged, but judg-

---

38   *Jacinta of Fatima*, Benoit Bemelmans, Crusade Magazine, July/August 2017, p. 8

ing himself — all his failings, all his unloving actions, and realizing that all the extraneous aspects of life, money, reputation, honor, power were as nothing.

Then Jesus took him on an extraordinary journey. He was shown people who had died but were still wandering the earth. One woman kept following a man, her son, and constantly nagging him; however, he could not see or hear her. George accompanied Jesus from city to city experiencing people in various conditions as a result of the lives they had lived. One young man followed an older man from room to room saying, "I'm sorry Pa! I didn't know what it would do to Mama. I didn't understand. I'm sorry Mama." He repeated this endlessly over and over again to ears that could not hear. There was a boy following a teenage girl through the corridors of a school. He kept saying, "I'm sorry, Nancy." There were examples of people trying to apologize to those who could not see or hear them. Jesus enlightened George, "They are suicides, chained to every consequence of their act."

They stopped at a bar where people were drinking and having fun. There were non-living men standing at the bar who were unable to lift the glasses to their lips. Over and over they kept trying to clutch the glasses, but their hands passed right through them.

Then George was taken to a plain which was crowded with ghostly beings. These thousands of people were the angriest, most frustrated, most completely miserable beings he had ever seen. They kept fighting, writhing, punching, were on top of each other, but no one was injured; it was like they were hitting the air. They could not kill each other because they were already dead; so they just hurled themselves at each other in a frenzied rage. Even more hideous were the sexual abuses many were performing in pantomime. Unimaginable perversions were being attempted in complete frustration. There was complete despair all around. It is interesting to note that George does not mention any fire as in the previous descriptions of hell. Read the rest of this fascinating true story that changed George's life forever.[39]

What does the Quran (Koran) say?

In the Muslim world, the Islamic Reformers explain that the Quran forbids suicide bombers. For such an evil act a Muslim will go to hell. Former Prime Minister of Pakistan Benazir Bhutto wrote, "In the Quran, preserving life is a central moral value. It does not permit suicide but demands the preservation of life." Islamic writers state, "The Prophet said: Whoever kills himself with blade will be tormented with that blade in the fires of Hell. . .He who throws himself off a mountain and kills himself will throw himself downward into the fires of Hell forever and ever. . . Whoever kills himself in any way will be tormented in that way in Hell."[40]

Does this mean that a suicide bomber who blew himself/herself up killing other people as well will blow himself/herself up over and over and over again in hell? What about those terrorists who, on September 11, 2001 crashed planes into the two World Trade Center Towers, the Pentagon, and Flight 93 where the heroic passengers prevented a worse disaster by crashing the plane in a field in Pennsylvania? Will those terrorists continue to crash the planes blowing themselves up over and over and over again for all eternity – a never-ending, never-ending punishment? How horrible is that?

Did God create hell?

These are only a very few of the people who have had visions of the horrors of hell. In the Bible it tells us "God looked at everything He

---

39   *Return from Tomorrow*, George G. Ritchie, Guideposts Edition
40   *Bin Laden: The Man Who Declared War On America*, Yossef Bodansky, p. xiii

had made, and He found it very good." (Genesis 1:31) Everything God created was *very good*. But what about hell? Did God create something that was not good? Is it possible that God did not create hell? If so, then who did; how did it come to be? In my readings I discovered an interesting concept: "We must make this abundantly clear: evil, suffering, death, and hell (that is eternal damnation in everlasting torment) *are not acts of God*. I want to expand on this point. One day Father Candido was expelling a demon. Toward the end of the exorcism, he turned to the evil spirit and sarcastically told him, 'Get out of here. The Lord has already prepared a nice, well-heated house for you!' At this the demon answered, 'You do not know anything! It wasn't He (God) who made hell. It was us. He had not even thought about it.' Similarly, on another occasion, while I was questioning a demon to know whether he had contributed to the creation of hell, I received this answer: 'All of us cooperated. . .' When I am told (by those who confuse predestination with God's providence) that God already knows who will be saved and who will be damned, and therefore anything we do is useless, I usually answer with four truths that the Bible spells out for us: God wants everyone to be saved; no one is predestined to go to hell; Jesus died for everyone; and everyone is given sufficient graces for salvation."[41]

What is the truth? Did God create hell or did Satan and his cohorts create it? Remember two things – all that God created is good, and Satan is the father of lies. So where does that leave us regarding this question? I don't know the answer. Is there anyone who does? I know one thing – I do not want to go there, and I am sure that you don't either.

---

41   *An Exorcist Tells His Story*, Gabriele Amorth, p. 22

Can one be saved from going to hell?

Hell is really bad news; but here is the good news – you don't have to go there. The choice is *yours*. That's right – *you get to choose*. How does one insure that he/she will not end up in this torturous dungeon of horrors? Again, as always, the answer is simple – *believe in God and obey His commandments.* If you have not been obeying His commandments, change your ways, turn away from your sins, and seek God's forgiveness. Will God forgive you no matter how many times you have sinned and no matter how scarlet your sins may be? Without question. God is all loving and His greatest attribute is that of His Divine Mercy. What is the best way to find His forgiveness? Go to God with a sincere heart, pray for forgiveness, make a firm promise to give up your sins, then find a minister, priest, rabbi, or whatever your religious affiliation happens to be and join a group, church, synagogue that will support you.

If you have no particular belief and would like to know more, ask the Holy Spirit to guide you, then look around. There are many places of worship. Go to some and see where you would be most comfortable. Try it for a while to see whether you would like to join the congregation. Talk to friends or acquaintances who could recommend a place of worship. Are you a little apprehensive about talking to someone about such a private matter? Why not check out the various GOD and religious programs on TV. There is a wonderful variety from different affiliations. This could help you find the best one for you.

God is merciful and desires each person's salvation. Remember this – we will all be held accountable for our offences whether we choose to believe it or choose to fool ourselves into believing that there is no God. Believing or not believing in something does not make it so. After all this, don't you think that it is so much easier to follow God's commandments?

Whatever you do, don't get discouraged and don't give up. That is one of Satan's favorite tools. If you find yourself slipping back into your old sinful habits, go back to God again. Remember that He is all Love and will always welcome you back again and again. Jesus says, "I tell you, there will likewise be more joy in heaven over one repentant sinner than over ninety-nine righteous people who have no need to repent." (Luke 15:7) God does not desire the destruction of any of His children. He loves each and every one of us <u>*unconditionally*</u>.

Does God have a plan?

Take a look around you. What do you see? Our Country is a mess. The whole world is even worse – all the hatred, greed, oppression of peoples, natural disasters, wars. There is the ever-present threat of a nuclear war which would cause much death and destruction. What can be done? Only God can put a stop to all this madness. How will He do that? According to heavenly apparitions and prophecies, God will give all humankind a **Warning –Illumination of Conscience** that will affect every person on the earth at the same time. Check out the Internet for yourself.

(See Appendix D – The Warning: Illumination of Conscience)

Chapter 4

The Irredeemable – Is Anyone Irredeemable?

What kind of evil is this?

Let's check these out:

Adolf Hitler – Dictator, Military Leader, German leader of the Nazi Party, Fuhrer of Germany from 1934 to 1945. He initiated fascist policies that led to World War II and the genocide known as the Holocaust resulting in the deaths of six million Jews and another five million noncombatants. He died by committing suicide.

Joseph Stalin – Soviet revolutionary and political leader, dictator, and Premier leader of the Soviet Union from 1941 to 1953. His autocratic government was responsible for mass repressions, hundreds of thousands of executions and millions of deaths through famines and labor camps. Stalin signed 357 proscription lists in 1937 and 1938 that ordered the execution of 40,000 people. He ordered huge-scale population transfers. Between 1941 and 1949 nearly 3.3 million people were deported to Syria and Central Asia with approximately 43% dying of disease and malnutrition. Ethnic groups were forcibly relocated causing estimates of hundreds of thousands to end up dying en route.

<u>Mao Tse-tung</u> – Military Leader of the Chinese Communist Party from 1935 to 1976. His reputation centers around the Great Leap Forward that began in 1958. Official Chinese sources suggest that 16.5 million people died in the Great Leap Forward. Jung Chang and Jon Halliday in their book *Mao: the Unknown Story* reported that 70 million people were killed by Mao including 38 million in the Great Leap Forward.

<u>Saddam Hussein</u> – President of Iraq, one of the most brutal tyrants in modern history, dictator who ruled Iraq with violence and fear for over thirty years. Saddam's regime brought about the deaths of at least 250,000 Iraqis. He committed war crimes in Iran, Kuwait, and Saudi Arabia. In December 2003 he was captured by American soldiers who found him hiding like a rat in a hole in the ground. He was put on trial by the Iraqi Special Tribunal. Charges included the murder of 148 people, torture of women and children, the illegal arrest of 399 others. On November 5, 2006 he was found guilty of crimes against humanity and was sentenced to death by hanging. Arrogant and defiant until the end, he was hanged on December 30, 2006.

<u>Osama bin Laden</u> – the mastermind who founded the terrorist group al-Qaeda admitted responsibility for the worst homeland attack launched against our United States of America on September 11, 2001 when four commercial aircraft were hijacked. Two planes were flown into the two towers of the World Trade Center in New York and one plane was flown into the Pentagon in Arlington, Virginia. The fourth plane was headed toward Washington, D.C. either toward the Capitol or the White House. However, upon learning about the attacks on the World Trade Center and the Pentagon, the passengers and crew members launched an attack against the hijackers. The plane crashed

in a field near Shanksville, Pennsylvania killing all aboard thus preventing the aircraft from reaching its intended target. Bin Laden was also responsible for other attacks around the globe. President George W. Bush pledged to get him "dead or alive." Bin Laden remained in hiding for almost ten years. Finally, the United States learned that he was in Abbottabad, Pakistan. President Barak Obama gave the go ahead, and on May 1, 2011 our U.S. Navy SEALs stormed the compound and bin Laden was shot and killed. His body was taken to a U.S. Carrier for DNA testing and proof positive identification. After observing proper Islamic procedure, his body was buried at sea so as not to have a memorial place for his followers. The Americans and other countries celebrated with jubilation and relief with a sense of justice for those killed by the bombings orchestrated by bin Laden.

Bashar al-Assad – President of Syria and Commander-in Chief of the Syrian army. Human rights groups have reported that his political opponents are routinely tortured, imprisoned, and killed. In June 2012, uprisings became a full-scale civil war. There were daily reports of killing of scores of civilians by government forces. In August 2013 he employed the use of chemical weapons against civilians. By 2016 it was estimated that there were 470,000 deaths in Syria. In 2017 more chemical weapons were used on civilians. The Khan Shaykhun chemical attack on the Syrian people was answered by President Donald J. Trump using missile strikes on a Syrian airbase.

ISIS – is the Islamic State in Iraq and Syria. They are an extremist militant group which emerged from radical Sunni jihadists in Iraq. They were founded in 2004 and in June 2014 declared itself a caliphate, a state governed in accordance with Islamic law by God's deputy on earth who is seen as the successor to the prophet Muhammad. ISIS claims responsibility for the Paris, France terrorist attacks where suicide bombings and shootings at cafes, bars, a rock concert, and stadium left 130 people dead on November 13, 2015. Terrorist attacks in Brussels left 34 people dead and 198 injured on March 22, 2017. ISIS wants to "purify" the world by killing infidels – Christians and Jews, and killing apostates – Shiite Muslims, 200 million of them. ISIS also inspires "lone wolf" suicide bombers in our country and other countries.

<u>Qasem Soleimani</u> – an Iranian major general, commander of Quds Force. According to President Donald J. Trump, Soleimani was responsible for planting thousands of roadside bombs in Iraq and Afghanistan. U.S. National Security Advisor Robert O'Brien explained that Soleimani "was plotting to kill, to attack American facilities, and diplomats, soldiers, sailors, airmen and Marines located at those facilities."[42] President Trump decided to act. On January 3, 2020 Soleimani's Airbus plane arrived at Baghdad International Airport. A Toyota Avalon and a Hyundai Starex were then taken by Soleimani and his companions and departed towards downtown Baghdad. An MQ-9 Reaper drone of the U.S. Air Force launched several missiles striking the convoy engulfing the two cars in flames and killing ten people including Soleimani. How does God view these terrorists?

<u>Abortionists</u> – including Dr. George Tiller, the baby killer, Dr. Kermit B. Gosnell, other abortion doctors, Planned Parenthood along with other abortion clinics, and so-called scientific research centers that destroy human babies in their embryonic state – all that translates into the murder of more than 63 million precious babies made in the image and likeness of God in our country alone, not to mention the untold numbers of aborted babies in other countries. This has been

---

42   Lubold, Gordon; Youssef, Nancy A.; Coles, Isabel (7 January 2020). *"Iran Fires Missiles at U.S. Forces in Iraq". The Wall Street Journal.*

a scourge of human sacrifice the likes and numbers of which have never been seen before in human history. How does one process these outrageous acts against a loving God, our Creator? How does God Himself view this murderous transgression against His all-holy Person on such a large scale? How will God deal with this tremendous amount of evil?

<u>Wuhan Coronavirus Pandemic</u> – Covid-19 was first reported in Wuhan, China in December 2019 and quickly spread throughout the world. As of March 10, 2023 the pandemic had caused more than 676 million cases and 6.9 million confirmed deaths. Vaccines have been approved and distributed in various countries. Treatments using antiviral drugs, preventive measures including social distancing, wearing masks, travel restrictions, lockdowns, quarantining, as well as other measures were taken to try to control conditions as best as possible to help prevent the spread of Covid-19. However, many questions remain as to how and why this happened. Was it an accident? Was it an experiment in creating a new virus that somehow went wrong? Was it a virus purposely created as a biological weapon? Who knows? Will we ever find the answer?

<u>Vladimir Putin</u> – In February 2022 under the direction of Russian President Vladimir Putin, Russia invaded Ukraine. Putin insisted that Ukraine was part of Russia. The Ukrainian people did not consider themselves part of Russia and under the leadership of Volodmyr Zelenskyy decided to defend their homeland. The results have been devastating. As of March 16, 2023, there have been at least 42,295 deaths including civilians, 58,479 non-fatal injuries, 15,000 missing people, 14 million displaced people, 140,000 buildings destroyed, and approximately $350 billion in property damage.[43] Why? Why all this destruction?

---

43   Reuters

These are just a small sample of all the evil that exists in our world and that has existed since the beginning of the world. I'm sure that if you checked out history, you would find many, many more.

Are all these people who have committed such horrible crimes against humanity and against God Himself irredeemable? Will an all-merciful God permit that? Let's see.

God *is* all-merciful – He is always ready to forgive even the most grievous offenses if we are truly sorry and ask for His mercy. However, the sin against the Holy Spirit will not be forgiven. What is the sin against the Holy Spirit? Jesus answers us, "but the blasphemy against the Spirit will not be forgiven. . .whoever says anything against the Holy Spirit will never be forgiven, either in this age or in the age to come." (Matthew 12:31-32) What does Jesus mean?

St. Augustine explains that the sin against the Holy Spirit specifically mentioned in the Gospel of Matthew is the sin of final unrepentance. This means that a person rejects God's grace and pardon up to and including the moment of death. This sin against the Holy Spirit is usually the culmination of many previous sins resulting in a gradual turning of the mind and will to the contempt for the grace of salvation. Wow! What a sorry situation that must be. Of all the sins that one could possibly commit, this has got to be the worst because once you reach that point of final unrepentance, there *is no turning back*.

The only possible exception that comes to mind is that of a person who has been in the state of grave sin, has a near-death experience, and is allowed to view the consequences of his/her state of soul. (Someone must have been praying for him/her.) This experience usually has a very profound effect, and the person repents and dramatically changes his/her life. But these experiences are rather rare and taking such a risk is not worth the gamble with the deck stacked so much against you. Stop for a minute and think about that. I mean *really* think about it. This is one thing you better believe; it could make an eternal difference. Are you willing to take that chance?

Mary C. Neal. M.D. – who was introduced earlier states in her book, *To Heaven And Back*, "I know with a profound certainty that it (the hall in her near-death encounter) represented the last branch point of life, the gate through which each human being must pass. It was clear that this hall is the place where each of us is given the opportunity to review our lives and our choices, and where we are each given a final opportunity to choose God or to turn away – for all eternity."[44] St. Faustina Kowalska and Blessed Anne Catherine Emmerich both confirm this fact expressing that God in His infinite mercy gives one last opportunity for the soul to choose or to reject God.

Who was the first to reject an all-loving God?

Isaiah tells about Lucifer and his sin of pride. "I will scale the heavens; Above the stars of God I will set up my throne...I will ascend above the tops of the clouds; I will be like the Most High! Yet down to the nether world would you go to the recesses of the pit!" (Isaiah 14:13-15) "Then war broke out in heaven; Michael and his angels battled against the dragon. Although the dragon and his angels fought back, they were overpowered and lost their place in heaven. The huge dragon, the ancient serpent known as the devil or Satan, the seducer of the whole world, was driven out; he was hurled down to earth and his minions with him." (Revelation 12:7-9)

Lucifer's pride caused him to desire to be like God. He rebelled against God and, along with his cohorts, lost his place in heaven. He became known as Satan. So great was his sin of pride that he became full of hate and jealousy toward humankind. Because of this he did

---

44   *To Heaven And Back*, Mary C. Neal, M.D. , Watterbrook Press, Division of Random House, Inc., New York, p. 73

and continues to do everything he can to cause people to sin against God so that they too will lose the place that God has reserved for them in heaven. How stupid and foolish of Satan and his crew to deliberately give up all the beauty, glories, and happiness of heaven for the ugliness, pain, and sorrow of the torturous eternal flames of hell. Don't you think that seems very stupid and foolish? All that because of foolish pride. You wouldn't want to take that risk, would you? I know that I wouldn't. Remember, it is never too late to repent of your sins no matter how bad you think they are until you close your eyes in death. Murderers have repented and received forgiveness from God. Remember Ted Bundy, Karla Faye Tucker, Dr. Bernard Nathanson who turned away from their murderous sins, repented, and sought God's forgiveness and mercy? In doing so they were able to save their soul and eventually get to heaven. God loves you and *waits* for you with open arms. Don't let fear or foolish pride keep you from God and deprive you of the eternal happiness of heaven.

Who else rejects God?

These are the people who refuse to believe that there is a God, the atheists. How could anyone even think that there is no God when we can see all the wonders that He has created right before our eyes? How else could all this wonder come about? If one does not want to believe in God, that is his/her choice. But why do they try to influence God-fearing people and try to destroy what we hold dear? They insist and even use the courts to remove anything relating to God from public institutions and public property to prayer in schools and at public meetings. Aren't we guaranteed by our Constitution the freedom to worship as we choose? Separation of Church and State means that the government cannot dictate or force a particular religion on the people. It does not mean that we must eradicate God from our Country. George Washington, our first President, dedicated our Country to God. Check out the history.

Then there are those who hate God? Why? This is usually because something traumatic may have happened in their life and they blamed God for it. Let me give you an example:

<u>Marcy</u> was 84 years old when I met her. She had a lot of medical problems and needed constant care. My sister Jean, was taking care of her. Marcy had been away from God for many years, and now she was nearing the end of her earthly life. Jean asked me to pray for her. I said that I would be willing to come and pray with her. Marcy agreed, but I think it was because she wanted someone to listen to her story – she wanted sympathy. Before I went to see her, I prayed to the Holy Spirit for guidance and to give me the words that He wanted her to hear since I never know what I am going to say in a case like this.

When I went to see Marcy, she told me her story. She had been married to a wonderful man. She was in her thirties, and they loved each other very much. Six months later he died. Of course, she was heartbroken. At first she tried to accept it. But she couldn't understand why God would take this wonderful husband away from her. Eventually her grief turned to bitterness toward God. She was angry with God and turned away from Him. Then she met her second husband. That was a disaster and ended up in divorce, more pain, and unhappiness. At the time I met her, she was married to her third husband, a nasty abusive man who treated her badly. I talked with Marcy and prayed with her but she remained obstinate. I told her that God knew all the pain that she had been through and was still in, and that He would not let her die being away from Him, that He would bring her back to Himself. She didn't believe me. Her third husband died very suddenly one day, and she was glad to be rid of him. She had him cremated and told the funeral director that she did not want his ashes. She said, "I don't care what you do with them." How very sad. I went to see her and to pray with her. Jean prayed with her, also.

One particular day, after praying to the Holy Spirit, I went to see her. I tried to convince her that God does love her. It wasn't working. So I said, "Let me ask you this – when you die, would you rather be in heaven with your first husband who was so good to you and loved you so much, or would you rather be in hell with the husband who abused you and was so mean to you? The choice is yours to go to heaven or to go to hell." She was stunned by my words, and so was I. I hadn't intended for those words to come out of my mouth, but they did. She couldn't say anything and neither could I. After I left her house, realizing what I had said and the sharpness of my words, I didn't feel too good about it. I certainly did not intend to hurt her. It was too late now. I couldn't take it back. Fortunately for me, she was not angry with me. She wanted me to go back to see her. I did go back and to my surprise she had decided that she wanted to see a priest. So I called Father Frank, a very nice young priest with a gentle manner. He was able to talk with her, hear her confession, and give her Jesus in Holy Communion. It wasn't long after that when the Lord called her home to Himself.

I guess sometimes a person needs to hear sharp words. The Holy Spirit really knows how to get even a stubborn person's attention, doesn't He? Did God go after Marcy? Yes! God in His mercy reached out to Marcy first through my sister Jean, then through me, and finally through Father Frank. She was able to make peace with a loving, merciful God. Did He bring her back to Himself? Yes! Did He heal all her hurts? Yes! Is He going after you? Yes! Will He do the same for you? Yes! Will He heal all your hurts? Yes! Allow Him into your heart and you will see.

Who are the presumptive?

They take God's mercy for granted. They presume that they can continue their life of sin and will get to heaven without true repentance. Don't tink that you can have a so-called good time for yourself, continue living a sinful llife and God will automatically forgive you without true repentance on your part. Don't fool yourself. It doesn't work that way. You can try to fool yourself, but you cannot fool God. He knows all. He knows what is in your heart. Remember that even with true repentance, you will still be held accountable for your transgressions. That is where purgatory comes in. All of us have to answer for the harm we have caused, the people we have hurt. Purgatory is God's merciful way for us to make up for our sins and finally get to heaven.

What is despair?

Despair is the loss of hope. Some people believe that their sins are so great that God will not forgive them. Some people have a difficult time even forgiving themselves. Despair was the sin of Judas. "Then Judas, who had handed Him over, seeing that Jesus had been condemned, began to regret his action deeply. He took the thirty pieces of silver back to the chief priests and elders and said, 'I did wrong to deliver up an innocent man!' They retorted, 'What is that to us? It is your affair!' So Judas flung the money into the temple and left. He went off and hanged himself." (Matthew 27:3-5) Did Judas end up in hell? He deeply regretted what he had done. He also despaired. He could be in hell; he could spend a long time in purgatory and eventually get into heaven. Only God knows the final fate of Judas.

There is no need for anyone to despair of God's mercy. God loves all His children unconditionally. He has forgiven those who have committed murder. All one needs to do is to sincerely repent of his/

her sinfulness, ask God for mercy, and make a firm resolution to give up his/her life of sin. God will not refuse a contrite and sincere heart. God truly is an all-loving and merciful God. No sin is greater than the mercy of God.

<u>Father Jose Maniyangat</u> – was born in Kerala, India on July 16, 1949. He was ordained a priest on January 1, 1975. Leaving out the details of his life, let's fast forward to Sunday April 14, 1985, the Feast of Divine Mercy. Father Jose was going to celebrate Mass at a mission church in the north part of Kerala. He was riding a motorcycle when an accident occurred. He was involved in a head-on collision with a jeep driven by an intoxicated man. Father was rushed to the hospital which was about 35 miles away. He died en route and his soul came out of his body. He saw his body being carried to the hospital where he was pronounced dead. He saw the people who were crying and praying for him. Father Jose met his Guardian Angel who said, "I am going to take you to heaven, the Lord wants to meet you and to talk with you." The angel also said that he wanted to show him hell and purgatory.

Hell was an awful sight. Father saw Satan and the devils, an unquenchable fire, worms crawling, people screaming, fighting, and being tortured by demons. All these sufferings were due to unrepented sins. There are seven levels of suffering according to the number and kinds of mortal sins committed in their earthly life. The souls were very ugly and cruel. The sins that convicted them were mainly abortion, homosexuality, euthanasia, hatefulness, unforgiveness, and sacrilege. The angel explained that if they had repented, they would have avoided hell and gone to purgatory. Also, some people who repent of these sins could be purified on earth through their sufferings. This way they can avoid purgatory and go straight to heaven. There were

The Irredeemable – Is Anyone Irredeemable?

priests and bishops who were in hell because they had misled people with false teaching and bad example.

Next Father Jose was escorted to Purgatory. There are also seven levels of suffering and unquenchable fire but far less intense than in hell. There was no quarreling or fighting. Their main suffering is their separation from God. Some of these people committed numerous mortal sins but they were reconciled with God before their death. Even though they are suffering, they are at peace knowing that they will one day be with God in heaven. These souls asked Father to pray for them.

His angel then escorted Father to heaven passing through a dazzling white tunnel. Father experienced an incredible amount of joy and peace. In heaven he heard the most beautiful music. The angels were singing and praising God. He saw all the saints, the Blessed Mother Mary, St. Joseph, and holy bishops and priests who were shining like stars. He met the Lord Jesus Who told him, "I want you to go back to the world. In your second life you will be an instrument of peace and healing to my people. You will walk in a foreign land and you will speak a foreign tongue. Everything is possible with My grace." The Blessed Mother then told him, "Do whatever He tells you. I will help you in your ministries." Heaven is so beautiful; there is so much peace and happiness. Words cannot express it. It exceeds a million times our imagination. Heaven is our real home; we are all created to reach heaven and enjoy God forever.

Father Jose came back to the world with his angel. His soul went back into his body which was in the morgue and he came back to life. His body needed blood transfusions and surgery to repair broken bones. After two months he was released from the hospital, but his doctor said that he would never walk again. He was unable to move. Another month went by. Then he heard a voice saying, "You are healed. Get up and walk." He felt peace and healing power. He immediately got up and walked praising and thanking God for the miracle. His doctor was amazed. He said, "Your God is the true God. I must follow your God." The doctor was Hindu and asked Father to teach him about our Church. After studying the faith, the doctor was baptized by Father and became Catholic.

Following a message from his Guardian Angel, Father Jose came to the United States on November 10, 1986 as a missionary priest. He has worked in Idaho and a number of parishes in Florida. He conducts a Eucharistic and charismatic-healing ministry on the first Saturday of each month. He has been invited to conduct a healing ministry in major cities in the United States as well as many other countries. Through his Eucharistic-healing ministry many people have been healed physically, spiritually, mentally, and emotionally. He also conducts a special healing service of the family tree in which effects from ancestral sins are blocked and healing takes place. Generational healing is needed when the effects from family sins linger. Doctors and medicines do not heal certain sicknesses caused by our family tree. Scripture says that these effects can linger for three to five generations.[45]

"The Lord, the Lord, a merciful and gracious God, slow to anger and rich in kindness and fidelity, continuing His kindness for a thousand generations, and forgiving wickedness and crime and sin; yet not declaring the guilty guiltless, but punishing children and grandchildren to the third and fourth generation for their father's wickedness!" (Exodus 34:6-7)

---

45   *Life After Death Experience*, Fr. Jose Maniyangat, Website: frmaniyangathealingministry.com

The Irredeemable – Is Anyone Irredeemable?

After learning about all these accounts of experiences:

The peace, happiness, wonders, of Heaven with a loving God, the angels, saints, family members, friends

The temporary sufferings of Purgatory provided by an all-loving and merciful God to atone for our repented sins, then spend eternity with Him in Heaven

The ugliness, cursing, fighting, grotesque demons taunting and torturing souls, unquenchable fire of Hell.

The choice is yours. ***Which would you choose?***

III
Why Suffering?
&
Why Forgiveness?

Chapter 1

Why Does God Allow Suffering?

Did God make a mistake?

When God created the Universe and all things in it, everything was good, beautiful, and perfect. "God looked at everything He had made, and He found it very good." (Genesis 2:7)

Then God created Adam and Eve, gave them all kinds of fruit and plants to eat, but told them not to eat the fruit of the tree in the middle of the garden, lest they die. Lucifer (Satan) being jealous of mankind took the form of a serpent. The serpent, being the most cunning of all animals, tricked the woman into eating the forbidden fruit. She in turn gave it to her husband to eat. Because they disobeyed God, they were banished from the beautiful Garden of Eden. Sickness, disease, and death entered the world. God said, "For you are dirt, and to dirt you shall return." (Genesis 3:19) Was God angry? Was He vengeful? Or was He compassionate toward His beloved mankind? How and why did God act as He did? Let's see.

Because of the sin of Adam and Eve, we inherit a sinful nature. Does this seem fair? Think about this. God gave us free will – to obey or not to obey as we so choose. Haven't we all disobeyed God at some point, actually many times, in our life? Aren't we guilty and deserving of banishment from God? God is all holy – no sin can stand before His face. Therefore, (maybe with the exception of sinless babies) we all deserve the eternal fires of hell.

Why did God curse the earth?

"Cursed be the ground because of you." (Genesis 3:17) God is Wisdom. He knows how to take a bad thing and make it better. God uses the deterioration of the land so that we may better understand the ugliness and consequences of sin. What are these consequences? The consequences of sin are twofold. First, there is the physical aspect – sickness, disease, suffering, and death of the body. Second, is the spiritual side – the death of the soul. What does this mean? St. John tells us, "Each person was judged according to his conduct. Then death and the nether world were hurled into the pool of fire, which is the second death; anyone whose name was not found inscribed in the book of the living was hurled into the pool of fire." (Revelation 20:13-15) What does St. John mean by the second death? This second death is the death of the soul which culminates in the eternal punishment due to our sins in the pool of fire – the everlasting fires of hell.

What is God teaching us?

By allowing sickness, disease, and death to come into the world, God shows us that all the anguish, suffering, and sorrow of this world are but a taste of the unpleasantness because of our sins. Sometimes, these ills are a direct result of our sins such as abuses of our body, guilt of the wrongs we have done, abuses afflicted on us by another person's sins, etc. You get the idea, don't you? We may have some relief from our sufferings and sickness by the use of medicines, psychological therapy, changes in our circumstances, spiritual healings, and the comfort of family members and friends. However, these consequences, while they give us a glimpse of the unpleasant results of sin, only last for a relatively short time. If we cringe at these physical illnesses, how much worse will be the horrors that last for eternity?

Is there escape from damnation?

Remember that God is all good and loving and does not desire the destruction of any of His beloved children. But God's justice demands that restitution be made for our sins. Our own sense of justice confirms that. Are, then, are we doomed? The greatest of God's attributes is that of His unfathomable mercy. So God devised a plan to save us. He decided that He, Himself, would pay the price for our sins in the person of Jesus Christ, His Divine Son. In the fullness of time, He would come down to earth to teach us how to live a good life, how to be kind and compassionate, to be merciful and forgiving, and then pay the ultimate price of His suffering and death for our sins. He would ransom us so that we may have eternal life. Wow! Think about it. Can there be any greater love than this?

Now let's get back to the discussion of our human sufferings on this earth. After the fall of Adam and Eve, conditions grew worse on the earth. Cain murdered his brother Abel. As the population of the earth grew, people began worshiping idols and became more and more depraved. All this was due to the influence of Satan and the demons that roamed the earth seeking the destruction of souls. Since very few righteous people were to be found, God decided to destroy the inhabitants of the earth. He commanded Noah, a righteous man, to build a huge ark so that he and his family and animals would be saved from the coming flood. Read the entire account of the great flood, the Deluge, starting in Genesis 6:5. Noah, his family, and all the animals that were in the ark were saved. But what happened to all the other people who drowned? Didn't God love them? Didn't He care about them? Couldn't they be saved? Were they utterly destroyed, body and soul? Blessed Anne Catherine Emmerich, an Augustinian nun who bore the stigmata, and is one of the greatest mystics and visionaries of the nineteenth century, tells us:

"There were frightful deeds upon the earth in those days. Men delivered themselves up to all kinds of wickedness, even the most unnatural. They plundered one another and carried off whatever suited them best, they laid waste homes and fields, they kidnapped women and maidens. . .they were deeply imbued with wickedness. They practiced the most shameful idolatry."[46]

Then, the rains came in torrents for forty days and forty nights. What happened to the souls of all the people who drowned? Blessed Anne Catherine goes on to tell us that the misery was so great, that it "was the means of many a soul's salvation." In the Bible God, Himself tells us, "Then call upon Me in time of distress, I will rescue you, and you shall glorify Me." (Psalm 50:15) "While He slew them they sought Him and inquired after God again, remembering that God was their rock and the Most High God their redeemer." (Psalm 78:34-35) This means that in their misery, they will call out to God and He will save them. How is He saving them when they end up dead? The body may be dead, but the soul lives forever. When they call out to Him, He saves their soul from eternal damnation. Therefore, when natural disasters occur such as earthquakes, tsunamis, volcanic eruptions, raging floods, and people cry out to God, He saves their souls.

---

46 *The Life of Jesus Christ And Biblical Revelations*, From the Visions of Anne Catherine Emmerich, as recorded by the journals of Clemens Brentano, Very Reverend Carl E. Schmoger, C.SS.R., Vol. 1 p. 34

Where was God in the face of such evil?

This question has been asked many times when six million Jews were exterminated by Hitler's henchmen. The holocaust was a very great evil perpetrated by an extremely evil man who used his God-given free will for human destruction and to feed his greed for power. Where was God at this horrendous time in Jewish history? Did God abandon His people?

Rabbi Harold S. Kushner gives us some insight into this question in his book, *When Bad Things Happen to Good People*. God gave us a free will meaning "that our being human leaves us free to hurt each other, and God can't stop us without taking away the freedom that makes us human. . .This line of reasoning helps me understand that monstrous eruption of evil we speak of as the Holocaust, the death of millions of people at the hands of Adolf Hitler. When people ask, 'Where was God in Auschwitz? How could He have permitted the Nazis to kill so many innocent men, women, and children?,' my response is that it was not God who caused it. It was caused by human beings choosing to be cruel to their fellow men." Some people say it was God's will. Rabbi Kushner continues, "I cannot make sense of the Holocaust by taking it to be God's will. . .the Holocaust represents too many deaths, too much evidence against the view that 'God is in charge and He has His reasons.' I have to believe that the Holocaust was at least as much of an offense to God's moral code as it is to mine, or how can I respect God as a source of moral guidance? Why did six million Jews, and several million other innocent victims, die in Hitler's death camps? Who was responsible? We fall back on the idea of human freedom to choose. . .free to choose to be good, which means he must be free to choose to be evil." Hitler chose to do evil, but he was not alone. It happened because thousands of others could be persuaded or frightened into joining him. Where was God when all this was going on? Why did He not intervene to stop it? Why didn't He strike Hitler dead in 1939 and spare millions of lives and untold suffering? Where was God? I have to believe that He was with the victims, and not with the murderers, but that He does not control man's choosing between good and evil. I have to believe that the tears and prayers of the victims aroused God's compassion, but having given Man freedom to choose, including the freedom to choose to hurt his neighbor, there was nothing God could do to prevent it,"[47]

Rabbi Kushner goes on to explain God's anguish and compassion at the suffering of innocent people and perhaps God cries with them, but He doesn't seem to do anything to help them because He will not infringe on humankind's free will.

I agree with Rabbi Kushner's premise up to the point of God's compassion of human suffering. However, I do believe that God indeed does do something about it. God *always* does what is best for each individual. Again we ask, did God abandon His people? God loves His children, all of them, and would never abandon them. Did He help them? Yes, He did. How did He help them when they were all dead? Going back to Blessed Anne Catherine Emmerich's explanation as to what happens when people are subjected to great sufferings and death – their misery was so great that they turned to God and it was a means of many a soul's salvation. God's main concern is for the *salvation of the soul* which lives forever. The body is only a temporary dwelling for the soul. During the Holocaust, in their misery a great many of these people must have called out to God, and in His mercy, He saved their souls. He *was* there for them. And He will *always* be there for you, too! Trust Him.

---

47   *When Bad Things Happen to Good People*, Harold S. Kushner, Anchor Books, Division of Random House, Inc., New York, 1981, pp.91-94

Did you see it on the news on television?

The people of Iraq were suffering all kinds of abuses at the hands of a ruthless dictator, Saddam Hussein. There were pictures of dead Iraqis with their throats cut, their eyes gouged out, jail cells with dried blood and rusty shackles bolted to the walls, torture chambers with instruments that depicted horrible atrocities inflicted on people suspected of anything that might be against the government. Mass graves were uncovered of tens of thousands of Kurds in the north and Shiites in the south, of people who were tortured and killed after Saddam seized power in 1979. Does anyone think that God didn't see this, that He didn't care about what was going on, that He abandoned these people? Remember that God is in control of all things. It was of God's intervention to free these people that President George W. Bush sent in the United States Military to clean out the evil over the objections of many U.S. citizens. You don't think that God had anything to do with this. Think again. He directs all things according to His will and according to what is *best* for the people. We as finite beings cannot know the wisdom of the infinite God. He heard the cries of these people, and He answered them. Today the Iraqi people are grateful to be rid of that evil regime and to be free.

But what about each individual Iraqi who was tortured and killed? A great many of them must have called out to God *as they knew Him*, and in His mercy, He must have saved their souls. A really loving and compassionate God would do that. If God was willing to come to earth in the person of Jesus Christ and suffer all the atrocities, humiliation, and die in excruciating pain on the cross to save us from the punishment that we deserve because of our sins, wouldn't He also be willing to save these people whom He loves? If you were God, wouldn't you? *God loves all His children!*

Chapter 2

Oh God, Why ME?

Who likes to suffer?

I am not good at suffering. I don't like any kind of pain at all – physical, emotional, psychological, spiritual, whatever – I don't like suffering. Do you? Jesus did not like to see people suffer either. He was loving and compassionate. He healed many people of their physical illnesses. He cast out demons, and healed their spiritual illnesses caused by sin and admonished them to sin no more. Jesus knew that many kinds of sins such as anger, resentment, guilt, unforgiveness, abuse of one's own body that are carried around for a long time manifest themselves as physical illnesses such as cancer, high blood pressure, heart disease, diabetes, and other debilitating illnesses. Jesus Himself did not like to suffer. In the garden of Gethsemane Jesus, knowing what was to befall Him, prayed, "My Father, if it is possible, let this cup pass Me by. Still, let it be as You would have it, not as I...Withdrawing a second time, He began to pray, 'My Father, if this cannot be done without My drinking it, Your will be done!...He began a third time, saying the same words as before." (Matthew

26:39,42,44) Three times Jesus begged His Father not to let Him go through this suffering and death on the cross. In the end, Jesus obeyed and accepted His Father's will.

What good comes out of suffering?

Jesus' suffering and death on the cross brought about salvation for all of us. Because of His great love, God Himself in the person of Jesus Christ, came down from heaven in the form of a human being, lived among us, and gave up His very life for us. He subjected Himself, the Lord of the Universe, to be born of the Virgin Mary, to be obedient to Mary and Joseph his foster father, as His human parents, and to grow under their authority. Wow! It must have taken a great amount of love and humility on the part of an all-powerful God to do that. Just think about that! Wait, we are not done yet. Jesus traveled around helping all kinds of people, Jews, Samaritans (not well liked by the Jews), Gentiles (pagans). Jesus came to serve, not to be served. "Such is the case with the Son of Man Who has come, not to be served by others, but to serve, to give His own life as a ransom for the many." (Matthew 20:28) He taught His disciples to serve. At the Last Supper, after washing the feet of the disciples, "Jesus said to them, 'Do you understand what I just did for you?. . .But if I washed your feet – I Who am Teacher and Lord – then you must wash each other's feet. What I just did was to give you an example: as I have done, so you must do.'" (John 13:12-15)

Then Jesus did an incredible thing. He instituted the Holy Eucharist. Exactly what does that mean? Jesus took ordinary bread and wine and changed it into His body and blood. It still keeps the appearance of bread and wine, but it actually becomes His body and blood. Many people have trouble believing that. Do you? If so, let me ask you this – do you believe that Jesus is God, the Second

Person of the Holy Trinity? Do you believe that God is the Creator and Master of the Universe and all that is in it? Do you believe that God can do anything? "Jesus looked at them and said, 'For man it is impossible; but for God all things are possible.'" (Matthew 29:26) Therefore, Jesus being God can change bread and wine into His body and blood. In addition, Jesus empowered His priests to do the same thereby leaving us His very self to be with us always. "And know that I am with you always, until the end of the world." (Matthew 28:20)

Now comes the most difficult part – the suffering. Jesus was betrayed by Judas Iscariot, one of His disciples. He was arrested and subjected to a so-called "trial." The chief priests and elders of the Sanhedrin secured false testimony against Him. He was mistreated and abused. Jesus was accused of blasphemy, declared guilty, the punishment for which is death. However, since according to them it was unlawful for them to put Him to death, they sent Him to Pontius Pilate, the Roman governor. After questioning Jesus, Pilate found no case against Him. The Jews were not satisfied; they wanted Jesus dead. "Pilate's next move was to take Jesus and have Him scourged. The soldiers then wove a crown out of thorns and fixed it on His head." (John 19:1-2) Pilate wanted to release Jesus, but due to pressure from the chief priests and elders, he decided to let the people choose – and they shouted, "Crucify Him!"

Can anyone even begin to imagine the suffering inflicted upon our loving Savior? He was physically assaulted, slapped in the face, spit upon, scourged, crowned with sharp thorns piercing His head, humiliated, mocked, and made to carry His own heavy cross which dug into His already bruised shoulder, to Calvary, the Place of the Skull. When they reached the place of crucifixion, the soldiers tore off His clothes which had adhered to His blood-stained skin causing unbearable pain. Then they threw Him down on the cross, stretched out His arms and legs dislocating the joints, and nailed Him to the cross causing excruciating pain. After raising the cross and securing it, Jesus had to hang there for three hours unable to move. In order to breathe, He had to push up with His nail-fastened feet. This sent waves of agonizing pain through His body. Lack of sufficient oxygen, extreme exhaustion, intense pain, burning thirst – no relief – and the knowledge that His Mother Mary had to stand there as part of this whole scene unable to offer any assistance or comfort.

All of Jesus' suffering was predicted in the Old Testament of the Bible. Read it for yourself, especially Isaiah Chapter 53. All this to pay the price for *our* sins so that *we* may have eternal life.

> **"Come, all you who pass by the way, look and see**
> **Whether there is any suffering like my suffering."**
> (Lamentations 1:12)

> **"There is no greater love than this:**
> **to lay down one's life for one's friends."**
> (John 15:13)

Why suffering, why Oh God?

Physical pain and suffering is present when the body is hurting. Moral suffering is the pain of the soul. Psychological pain and suffering accompanies both moral and physical pain which is manifested in sadness, disappointment, discouragement, or even despair.[48] The result of the moral evil of sin is punishment. God is a Just Judge Who rewards good and punishes evil. However, God being all-merciful, took upon

---

48 *On The Christian Meaning Of Human Suffering,* Salvifici Doloris, Apostolic Letter, Pope John Paul II, 1984, pp. 3, 5

Himself our sins in the person of Jesus Christ His only begotten Son. Without His doing so, we would be condemned to hell. Jesus paid the price for our sins, but we will still be held accountable for them. If Jesus paid the price for our sins, why will we be held accountable for them? *Justice requires it.* God will pardon our sins providing we turn away from them and ask His forgiveness. God has provided a temporary place of reckoning, Purgatory, for us before we can get into heaven because nothing unholy can enter into His holy abode.

Why do the innocent suffer?

Not all suffering is punishment for sin. In the Book of Job in the Old Testament of the Bible, we read about an innocent man who undergoes much suffering. Yet he remains faithful to God. Why is that? "The Book of Job poses an extremely acute way of suffering; it also shows that suffering strikes the innocent, but does not give the solution to the problem."[49] In the Old Testament, the sufferings inflicted by God on the chosen people are not just a punishment for sin, but were meant not for the ruin but for the correction of the nation. It is in fact, a great kindness to punish sinners promptly instead of letting them go for long "that their sins may become worse requiring a more severe punishment later." (2 Maccabees 6:12-13)

Suffering creates the possibility of rebuilding goodness. An example of this is the August and September 2017 devastating effects of hurricanes Harvey, Irma, and Maria and the earthquakes in Mexico. These caused much damage, loss of homes, loss of employment, possibility of diseases, and even death. Also, the more recent effect of Corona-virus Covid-19 which caused much sickness and millions of deaths all over the world. The people have and are still suffering tremendously. Does *any* good come out of this? Yes, it does. "This

---

49   Ibid, p. 10

is an extremely important aspect of suffering. . .Suffering must serve for conversion, that is, for the rebuilding of goodness in the subject (person) who can recognize the divine mercy in this call to repentance. The purpose of penance is to overcome evil. . .and to strengthen goodness both in man himself and in his relationships with others and especially with God. . .Love is also the fullest source of the answer to the question of the meaning of suffering. . .given by God to man in the cross of Jesus Christ."[50] "Yes, God so loved the world that He gave His only Son that whoever believes in Him may not die but may have eternal life. God did not send His Son into the world to condemn the world, but that the world might be saved through Him." (John 3:16-17) Through all this suffering many people stepped up and did heroic service to help all those suffering people. Did God see all this? You bet He did, and I am sure He was very pleased to see the love and kindness of so many people helping those in need.

What is redemptive suffering?

Suffering comes to everyone sooner or later. No one is exempt. I don't like suffering, do you? Does anyone? Is there anything good that comes from personal suffering? Believe it or not, there is. When a person is sick or suffering in some way, Catholics are taught to "offer it up." Offer it up? What does that mean? Offer it up to whom? You offer your sufferings to God. Now to Protestant Christians that may seem rather strange. What is the purpose of offering it up? Didn't Jesus suffer to redeem us from our sins so that we may have eternal life? Yes, of course, He did. St. Paul tells us, "Even now I find my joy in the suffering I endure for you. In my own flesh I fill up what is lacking in the sufferings of Christ for the sake of His body, the Church." (Colossians 1:24) What is lacking in the sufferings of Christ? There

---

50   Ibid, pp. 10-11

is nothing lacking in the sufferings of Christ. So what does this mean? God wants to share *everything* with us. He allows us to share in His creative power not only using our imagination and ingenuity to make something, or paint a beautiful picture, or do some creative writing, but in our own body by creating another human being. How awesome is that! He wants us to share our thoughts, our feelings, and our pain with Him. And He wants to share with us, in the person of Jesus, His life, teachings, sufferings, death, resurrection, and glory in heaven. God wants to be completely one with us. The Holy Spirit reproduces all this in us.

But is there more?

Redemptive suffering has value. When we offer up our suffering united to the sufferings of Jesus, we can help bring grace to others that they may accept God's gift of salvation. We can help the souls in purgatory get into heaven sooner. No one likes to suffer. Jesus didn't like it either. In fact, Jesus dreaded having to go through His passion and death. In the garden of Gethsemane, Jesus prayed, "My Father, if it is possible, let this cup pass Me by. Still, let it be as You would have it, not as I." (Matthew 26:39) "In the days when He was in the flesh, He offered prayers and supplications with loud cries and tears to God, Who was able to save Him from death, and He was heard because of His reverence. Son though He was, He learned obedience from what He suffered; and when perfected, He became the source of eternal salvation for all who obey Him." (Hebrews 5:7-9) Jesus didn't like suffering either for Himself or for others. He was just as human as the rest of us.

Remember, God Himself, because of His great love for us, came to earth, in the person of Jesus Christ, suffered and died for each and every one of us so that we may have eternal life. He came not only for you and for me but for each and every person in the entire world regardless of race, creed, where we came from, who our family members might be, how much money we have or don't have, or whatever else you might consider. No one, **no one** is excluded. If a person does not achieve eternal salvation, it is because he/she *refuses God's grace* ***by choice***. Jesus was obedient and accepted His suffering and death for our sake. Most people do not want suffering, and they will do almost anything to avoid it. For example, some turn to alcohol and drugs to bury the pain in their life instead of confronting it. Jesus tells us, "If a man wishes to come after Me, he must deny his very self, take up his cross and begin to follow in My footsteps." (Matthew 16:24) In other words, we must be willing to accept our cross – accept our sufferings. How do we do that? Actually, the hardest part is to give up control. We are used to coming and going as we please, to doing whatever we want. But when sufferings come over which we have no control, how do we act? Do we become angry, frustrated, depressed? Do we take out our feelings on others? However, when we offer it up to God, when we accept it, we give control over to God. Does that mean we don't try to get medical help, or whatever help we may need? Not at all. We seek the help we need and follow the advice of professionals. Then we put it in God's hands and let Him handle it. God then gives us the strength to bear our sufferings. Know that He will not allow us to be taxed beyond our endurance. His grace is sufficient to see us through it all.

As a material witness to her Son's passion and death on the cross, Mary played a special role as co-Redemptrix by her intense and unimaginable suffering that a mother could experience. Standing at the foot of the cross, in addition, she became the spiritual mother to us all when Jesus said to His disciple, "There is your mother." (John

19:27) Because of her willingness and suffering, many souls are saved through Mary's intercession.

What is redemptive power?

When we unite our sufferings to the sufferings of Jesus, it is transformed by the Holy Spirit into redemptive power and made useful for God. It can help save souls, and it can help the souls in purgatory get to heaven sooner. There are many saints who offered their redemptive suffering for the salvation of souls and for the souls in purgatory. Blessed Anne Catherine Emmerich, St. Padre Pio, St. Francis of Assisi, all of whom bore the stigmata (wounds of Christ), no doubt saved many souls by their prayers and sufferings. St. Pope John Paul II toward the end of his life was an outstanding example and a beacon of hope for those suffering with serious illnesses. There are many canonized saints as well as saintly people (victim souls) who offer up their sufferings united to the sufferings of Jesus. "Every man has his own share in the redemption. Each one is called to share in that suffering through which all human suffering has also been redeemed. In bringing about the redemption through suffering, Christ has also raised human suffering to the level of redemption. Thus each man in his suffering can also become a sharer in the redemptive suffering of Christ."[51]

So what is the bottom line of suffering?

"Down through the centuries and generations it has been seen that in suffering there is concealed a particular power that draws a person interiorly close to Christ, a special grace. To this grace many saints...and others owe their profound conversion...the individual discovers

---

51 *On The Christian Meaning Of Human Suffering*, Salvifici Doloris, Apostolic Letter, Pope John Paul II, 1984, p. 21

the salvific meaning of suffering...He discovers a new dimension, as it were, of his entire life and vocation...Christ through His own salvific suffering is very much present in every human suffering and can act from within that suffering by the powers of His Spirit of Truth,...Faith in sharing in the suffering of Christ brings with it the interior certainty that the suffering person 'completes what is lacking in Christ's afflictions'...It is suffering, more than anything else, which clears the way for grace which transforms human souls... suffering is present in the world in order to release love, in order to give birth to works of love toward neighbor, in order to transform the whole of human civilization into a civilization of love...Christ has taught man to do good by His suffering and to do good to those who suffer. In this double aspect He has completely revealed the meaning of suffering."[52]

---

52 Ibid, pp. 31-33, 38, 39

Chapter 3

Why Forgiveness?

Are you responsible and must you stand alone?

Are you alone responsible for your sins? Yes, you are responsible and you will be held accountable. Since you have free will, you cannot blame anyone else for your sins. But before you can accept responsibility, you must first realize that you have sinned. An example would be an alcoholic. Before he/she can be healed, the realization of having the disease must come. It started with the first drink and gradually escalated into an addiction. The healing process will also take some time. Sometimes, as is the case with an addiction, there are circumstances which lessen the responsibility but does not take it away. It may take some time to fully realize your sin, but ultimately, you need to seek forgiveness from God and to forgive yourself.

Are you truly sorry?

In order to have forgiveness from God, you must be truly sorry for offending Him. How do you know if you are truly sorry for your sin? Are you willing to completely give up your sin? If so, then you are truly sorry. True contrition for sin involves the willingness to change – a sincere commitment to "sin no more." Is there more that must be done? Yes. Depending on the sin, every effort must be made to right the wrong. For example, if something had been stolen, it must be returned; if lies were told, the truth must be made known. But what if you commit the same sin again? God will always forgive you if you are truly sorry and ask His help to overcome your sin. Habitual sins can be difficult to overcome because of human weakness. With God's help, however, you can overcome any sin.

How do you know that you are forgiven?

God always forgives the truly repentant sinner. Sometimes a person is riddled with guilt even though he/she has truly repented. This means that he/she has not forgiven himself/herself. Guilt is a tool that Satan uses to enslave people. There is no need to carry guilt once a person has made a commitment to avoid further sin. Catholics confess their sins to a priest who represents Christ. The priest gives absolution whereby all their confessed sins are forgiven and taken away. Jesus gave His priests the power to forgive sins when He said, "Receive the Holy Spirit, If you forgive men's sins, they are forgiven them; if you hold them bound, they are held bound." (John 20:23) Other religious faiths believe in confessing their sins only to God. However, confessing one's sins to another person such as a priest, minister, rabbi has a tremendous therapeutic effect in helping a person to know that he/she is truly forgiven and greatly diminishes or eliminates the sense of guilt. When we truly repent of our sins, God, Himself, tells us in the Bible, "As far as the east is from the west, so far has He put our transgressions from us." (Psalm 103:12) Not only that but God says he will *forget* our sins. "It is I, I Who wipe out, for My own sake, your offenses; your sins I remember no more." (Isaiah 43:25)

Would you like to know how God forgets your sins?

Quite a number of years ago, my neighbor and I were really close friends, and we shared many beautiful thoughts together. And then something happened between us that completely destroyed our friendship. This was very painful to me. After a while, through prayer and anguish of heart, we were able to get to the place where we were once more on friendly terms. I felt that I had truly forgiven her and hoped that she felt the same way. Then one March day, I happened to be reading the newspaper, the Dear Abby column, where a woman had written saying that she had a friend who had done a lot of things to hurt her. She wrote that she had forgiven this friend, but somehow she could not forget all those hurtful things. Abby's reply was, "If you can't forget, then you haven't really forgiven." I thought about that. Having a sharp memory, I could remember all the things that happened between my neighbor and me as they were still fresh even though I did not dwell on them. In the Bible the Lord says, "...I will forgive their evildoing and remember their sin no more." (Jeremiah 31:34) So I asked the Lord, "Lord, how is that possible? I know You forgive my sins when I am sorry for them, but how can You *forget* my sins, You Who are God and know all things? Me, in my humanness, I can remember all this so vividly, how can *You* forget my sins? I do not understand, Lord. Please teach me." And so the Lord proceeded to teach me.

The first thing the Lord did was to speak to my heart and my mind, and He said. "Would you be willing to be friends with her again?" I said, "Yes, Lord, I would be willing to be friends with her again." He left me at that point for about three days. Then the Lord came back to me and said, "Would you be willing to have her visit you and share a cup of coffee with you?" I replied, "Yes, Lord, I would be willing to do that." Again, the Lord left me at that point for about a week or so. Then the Lord came back and said, "Would you be willing to share confidences and personal things with her again?" And I said, "Oh, wait a minute, Lord. That's asking a little too much. How could I possibly do that? No, Lord. I'm sorry. That would be too difficult, so awkward. I can't do that, Lord." The Lord accepted that and left me at that point for about two weeks.

After two weeks, the Lord came back and said, "Would you be willing to share confidences with her again?" I said, "Lord, You know that I love You above all else, and I will do anything You ask of me, but how could I possibly do this?" And the Lord said, "Trust Me." So I said, "OK, You got it, Lord. But if You really and truly want me to get to the point where we can again share personal things and confidences, then You're going to have to do it because I can't. It would be so awkward for me to go to her. How could I do this. I don't know how, Lord. You are going to have to do it." And the Lord said, "Good enough."

Then I began to realize that something amazing was happening to me all this time, this process that the Lord was taking me through. I was forgetting all the pain that had taken place. But more importantly I had no *desire* to remember all those things. The desire to bring it all up again was completely gone. Then it was that I was able to understand that, yes, it is possible when you really and truly forgive, you really and truly forget. I understood how it was possible for the Lord to forgive my sins and to completely forget my sins – He has no *desire* to remember my sins. How wonderful that really is!

There was one thing that bothered me. Sometimes relatives or friends would say, "Well that's nice that you are back on friendly terms, but don't get too friendly, just keep it casual." Every time I would hear this, I would cringe because to me that was not a true forgiveness. I knew that these people meant well. They loved me so much that they didn't want to see me hurt again.

Anyway, the Lord wasn't finished with me yet. About a month later, in April, I read in the newspaper that my neighbor's mother died. I was stunned because I didn't even know that she was sick. I sent my neighbor a nice card with a note saying, "Your mother was such a generous and warm and beautiful person, and I loved her. Know that my prayers are with you in your time of sorrow." About a week after that I saw her, we exchanged a few words, and she thanked me for the card. Then in June she had been in the hospital, and again I hadn't known anything about it until a little later. Figuring that she must really be hurting, I continued to pray for her.

Then one day in September, it was a beautiful day so I went outside in my back yard, and she happened to be out hanging clothes. I went over and started talking to her. She shared with me about her mother's death and her own illness in the hospital. We also shared some very beautiful and personal things. I could see how much she was hurting, so I just put my arms around her, and I shared her tears. It was so beautiful. Just before I went back into my house, she said, "Why don't you come over and have a cup of coffee with me sometime." I extended the same invitation to her. I went into my house and thanked God for the beautiful, beautiful gift that He had given us that we could again share such beautiful and personal things together.

Sometimes, it is very difficult for a person to become reconciled with someone who has hurt you even though you have forgiven the person. Father Matthew Linn, S.J. whom I had seen a number of times at the Catholic Charismatic Conference in Scranton, Pennsylvania, gives a remedy for difficult forgiveness. Father would ask, "Do you forgive that person who hurt you?" And the person would say, "No, I don't forgive her." Father would continue, "Well, why don't you forgive her?" And the answer would usually be, "Because I have no desire to forgive her." Father would say, "OK" and accepts the person right where she's at just as Jesus would do. Again, Father would pursue the issue, "Would you be willing to be willing to forgive her?" In other words, if you are not willing to forgive that person now because it is perhaps too difficult, would you at least be willing to have the *desire* to forgive even though you do not have it now?" The person will almost always say, "Yes."

If a person is unwilling to forgive, it's not that the person is being stubborn. It's just that the hurt is so deep, she just doesn't know how to forgive; she doesn't know how to go about doing it. When she says, "No" that she has no desire to forgive, then the door to her heart is shut tight and the Lord's light cannot get in. But if she is at least willing to be willing to have the desire to forgive, then that's like a tiny crack in the door. No matter how tiny that crack is, the Lord's light can begin to shine through. Jesus is like that. He doesn't say, "Well, I'll meet you half way." He doesn't ever say, "You take the first step and then I'll come." No, He comes right to us and meets us right where we are because sometimes we don't know how to take that first step. But as long as we have the desire to take the first step, the Lord will take our hand and lead us. He will say, "Come, I will show you the way. I will teach you because I am the way, the truth, and the life."

Chapter 4

Why Should I Forgive?

What did Jesus do first?

Jesus was brutally beaten, crowned with thorns, mocked, spit upon, dragged into the street, and made to carry His own cross until Simon of Cyrene was forced to help Him for fear that He would die on the way. "When they came to the Skull Place, as it was called, they crucified Him there and the criminals as well, one on His right and the other on His left. Jesus said, 'Father forgive them; they do not know what they are doing.'" (Luke 23:33-34) Jesus, the Son of the Eternal Father, asked for forgiveness for His murderers. That was the first thing He did. He did not hesitate; He did it immediately; He did not have to think about it; He just did it. This is a wonderful example of how we should forgive those who hurt us.

Was Jesus done forgiving or was there more?

After Jesus forgave those responsible for His crucifixion, He again extended forgiveness. "One of the criminals hanging in crucifixion blasphemed Him: 'Aren't You the Messiah? Then save Yourself and us.' But the other one rebuked him: 'Have you no fear of God, seeing you are under the same sentence? We deserve it, after all. We are only paying the price for what we've done, but this Man has done nothing wrong.' He then said, 'Jesus, remember me when You enter upon Your reign.' And Jesus replied, 'I assure you: this day you will be with Me in paradise.'" (Luke 23:34-43) Wow! What a promise Jesus gave to this criminal who was crucified with Him. What kind of promise does Jesus give to each one of us? Let's find out.

Was there still more forgiveness to be had from Jesus?

Peter had denied that he even knew Jesus three times. "At the very moment he was saying this, a cock crowed. The Lord turned around and looked at Peter, and Peter remembered the word that the Lord had spoken to him, 'Before the cock crows today you will deny Me three times. He went out and wept bitterly.'" (Luke 22:60-62) Peter was deeply sorry for his sin, but he still needed healing. So after Jesus' resurrection, at the Sea of Tiberias, Jesus took care of it. "When they had eaten their meal, Jesus said to Simon Peter, 'Simon, son of John, do you love Me more than these?' 'Yes, Lord,' he said, 'You know that I love You.' At which Jesus said, 'Feed My lambs.' A second time He put His question, 'Simon, son of John, do you love Me?' 'Yes, Lord,' Peter said, 'You know that I love You.' Jesus replied, 'Tend My sheep.' A third time Jesus asked him, 'Simon, son of John, do you love Me?' Peter was hurt because He had asked a third time, 'Do you love Me?' So he said to Him, 'Lord, You know everything. You know well that I love You.' Jesus said to him, 'Feed by sheep.'" (John 21-15-17) Three times Peter had denied Jesus, and three times Jesus extended forgiveness and healing to Peter. Since Peter was to be the chief shepherd after Jesus was to ascend into heaven, Jesus made it clear that He wanted Peter in that position, and Peter had to know that he was truly forgiven in order to handle that position properly. Without this healing, Peter may have had his doubts as to exactly what the Lord expected of him. Sometimes it is difficult for us to know what the Lord expects of us. However, if we trust Him, He will reveal to us what we need to know.

Why is it important to forgive?

Simply put – forgiveness brings healing in two ways:

First, when a person who has hurt another person is forgiven, he is relieved. The sense of guilt is much diminished or eliminated, and he can move on from that situation. If forgive-ness is not extended and the emotion of guilt is perpetuated, carrying the burden of guilt especially for a long period of time leads to physical illness.

Second, when the person who has been hurt forgives the offender, he removes a huge burden from himself. If left to carry a burden of unforgiveness, this gives rise to many types of illness from something as simple as frequent colds to very serious illnesses such as cancer. This happens because negative emotions, such as anger and hurt feelings causing one to be unable to forgive, depress the immune system leaving one open to many types of illness. Therefore, it is highly beneficial for each party to the hurt to seek forgiveness and healing.

If you or someone you know is having a difficult time with forgiving someone who caused hurt or injury, seek help from a professional. Members of the clergy as well as psychologists are especially good at this. People in the Prayer Ministry attest to the fact that when a person asks to be prayed with for healing, many times their physical pain is not relieved until they recite the Prayer of Forgiveness. The person is asked to forgive someone against whom he/she held a grudge. The pain disappeared when the person prayed to forgive the one who hurt him/her.

What effect does it have on you?

Research has found that forgiving someone and letting go of grudges has a beneficial effect on the heart and immune system. "When you hold a grudge, you're isolated in your suffering. The long-term damage to the cardiovascular system from bitterness and resentment is clearly established," says Fred Luskin, Ph.D., author of *Forgive for Good*, and the director of the Stanford Forgiveness Project. Dr. Luskin also found that forgiveness lowered stress, boosted feelings of self-confidence, and helped a person to feel a greater sense of community with other people. Also, fewer headaches, backaches, and upset stomachs were reported. Unforgiveness, whether you realize it or not, stays with you. It is always in the back of your mind. Your mental state affects your physical state. Unforgiveness may cause distress, anxiety, depression which affects your immune system that over an extended period of time can lead to many types of diseases. Who needs that?

What are the Ten Components of Forgiveness?

1. Forgiveness is not easy.
2. Forgiveness is not forgetting.
3. Forgiveness does not overlook evil.
4. Forgiveness is not indifference.
5. Forgiveness is not the same as approval.
6. Forgiveness recognizes and admits that people are bigger than their faults.
7. Forgiveness allows the offending person to start over again.
8. Forgiveness recognizes the humanity of the wrongdoer.
9. Forgiveness cancels the right to get even.
10. Forgiveness wishes the wrongdoer well.

Did you ever watch the popular TV show *NCIS*? Special Agent Gibbs has a saying, "Never say you're sorry. It's a sign of weakness." Is it? I don't think so. Rather, is it not a sign of foolish pride? It takes a person of strong character and humility to admit that he/she is wrong and to apologize. And, it takes a person of great humility to apologize when he/she knows he/she is right. Foolish pride has been the destruction of many good relationships. The best-known is that of Lucifer whose foolish pride estranged him from God. Where did that get him? He lost his position as one of God's most beautiful and brightest angels. He lost all the beauty and wonders of heaven. He took with him all his cohorts to live in the torments of hell forever. Was it worth it? Hell, NO!

What horrible evil is this?

On October 2, 2006, Charles Carl Roberts backed his pickup truck to the front of an Amish one-room schoolhouse in Nickel Mines, Lancaster County, Pennsylvania. He then went into the school and asked the teacher, Emma Mae Zook, and students ranging in age from six to thirteen, if they had seen a clevis pin along the road. After they denied seeing the object, Roberts went back out to his truck and returned to the classroom holding a 9mm handgun. He ordered the male students to carry several items from his truck into the classroom. Ms. Zook and her mother, who had been visiting the schoolhouse, escaped and ran to a nearby farm for help. Amos Smoker called 911.

Roberts barricaded the front door using wood boards that he had the male students carry into the school-house. After ordering the female students to line up against the chalkboard, he then allowed a pregnant woman, three parents with infants, and all the male students to leave the building. One female student escaped by following her brother out the door. Ten female hostages remained inside the building. Roberts then bound the arms and legs of his hostages with plastic ties.

Police and medical personnel arrived at the scene. Roberts warned them to leave immediately threatening to shoot the hostages. Police officers backed away, but did not leave. State police briefly established phone contact with Roberts, but to no avail as he continued to threaten to harm the girls. Then, Roberts began shooting the victims. As the state troopers immediately approached the window, the shooting suddenly stopped. Roberts had committed suicide. Three girls died at the scene. The rest were taken to medical facilities for treatment. Two more girls died the next morning. Most of the girls, ages six to thirteen, were shot execution style in the back of the head. The schoolroom was splattered with blood and glass over all the desks and chairs. Bullet holes were everywhere. Some of the girls had been shot with a 12-gage shotgun.

How did the Amish community respond to such horrendous evil?

The day of the murders, the grandfather of one of the girls killed said, "We must not think evil of this man." A father stated, "He had a mother and a wife and a soul and now he's standing before a just God." Jack Meyer, who lives near the Amish community explained that "the Amish people only wanted to *forgive* and reach out to those who have suffered including the family of the man who committed these acts." Only hours after the shooting, an Amish neighbor comforted the Roberts family and extended forgiveness to them. Members of the Amish community visited and comforted Marie Roberts, Charles' widow, his parents, and family members. To comfort him, one Amish man held Roberts' sobbing father in his arms for about an hour. The Amish people set up a charitable fund for the Roberts family. About thirty Amish people attended Roberts' funeral. Marie Roberts, an outsider, was invited to attend the funeral of one of the victims.

What was the effect on the Roberts family and on everyone watching this scene unfold?

Marie Roberts wrote a letter to the Amish community saying, "Your love for our family has helped to provide the healing we so desperately need. Gifts you've given have touched our hearts in a way no words can describe. You compassion has reached beyond our family, beyond our community, and is changing our world, and for this we sincerely thank you."

The West Nickel Mines Schoolhouse was demolished the following week and the scene left as a peaceful field. At a different location near the site, a new schoolhouse was built. It was called the New Hope School, and was intentionally built as "different as possible" from the original schoolhouse.[53] The compassion, generosity, and immeasurable spirit of forgiveness of the Amish people is truly remarkable. Only God Himself in His goodness and mercy surpasses such an incredible outpouring of love and compassion. Is it any wonder that these beautiful people possess such tranquility evident in their day to day living that most of us can only long for?

Do you want that kind of peace in your life? Why not try living a more simple lifestyle – not trying to keep up with the Joneses, being compassionate toward the needs of others and helping where you can, forgiving those who hurt you, and most of all keeping God's commandments. (See Appendix A – The Ten Commandments) "Blest too the peacemakers; they shall be called the sons of God." (Matthew 5:9)

---

53 *Amish school shooting*, Wikipedia

St. Paul exhorts us, "Rejoice in the Lord always! I say it again. Rejoice! Everyone should see how unselfish you are. The Lord is near. Dismiss all anxiety from your minds. Present your needs to God in every form of prayer and in petitions full of gratitude. Then God's own peace, which is beyond all understanding, will stand guard over your hearts and minds, in Christ Jesus." (Philippians 4:4-7)

Do you have trouble forgiving?

I came across this prayer. I don't know who wrote it, but it offers a way for you to free yourself from someone or something that needs to be forgiven. Read through it. It covers a lot, much of what may not even apply to you. You can adapt it to your own situation or add to it whatever else you might need.

<u>The Forgiveness Prayer</u>

Heavenly Father, I ask today to forgive everyone in my life. I know that You will give me strength to forgive. I thank You that You love me more than I love myself and want happiness more than I desire it for myself.

Father, I want to be free from the feelings of resentment, bitterness, and unforgiveness toward You for the times I thought You sent death, hardships, financial difficulties, punishments, and sickness into our family.

I forgive *myself* for my sins, faults, and failings. For all that is truly bad in myself or all that I think is bad, I do forgive myself. I forgive myself for delving into the occult, Ouija boards, horoscopes, seances, fortune telling, lucky charms. I forgive myself for taking Your name in vain, for not worshipping You, for hurting my parents, for getting drunk, for us-

ing drugs, for sins against purity, for adultery, for abortion, for stealing, and for lying. Thank You, Heavenly Father, for Your grace at this moment.

I forgive my *mother* for all the times she hurt me, resented me, was angry with me, and for all the times she punished me. I forgive her for all the times she preferred my brothers and sisters to me. I forgive her for the times she told me I was dumb, stupid, the worst of the children, or that I cost the family a lot of money. For the times she told me I was unwanted, an accident, a mistake, or not what she expected, I forgive her.

I forgive my *father* for any non-support, lack of love, affection, or attention. I forgive him for any lack of time, for not giving me his companionship, for his drinking or arguing and fighting with my mother or the other children. For his severe punishments, for desertion, for being away from home, for divorcing my mother or for any running around, I do forgive him.

Heavenly Father, I extend forgiveness to my *sisters and brothers*, those who rejected me, lied to me, hated me, resented me, competed for my parents' love, who hurt me, who physically harmed me. For those who were too severe on me, punished me or made my life unpleasant in any way, I do forgive them.

I forgive my *spouse* for lack of love, affection, consideration, support, attention, communication, for faults, failings, weaknesses, and those other acts or words that hurt or disturb me.

I forgive my *children* for their lack of respect, obedience, love, attention, support, warmth, and understanding. I forgive them for their bad habits, falling away from the Church, and any bad actions which disturb me.

My God, I forgive my *in-laws* and other relatives by marriage for their lack of love, words of criticism, thoughts, actions, or omissions which injure or cause pain, I do forgive them.

Please help me to forgive my relatives who may have interfered in our family, been possessive, who may have caused confusion or turned one parent against the other.

Lord Jesus, help me to forgive my *co-workers* who are disagreeable or make life miserable for me. I forgive those who push their work off on me, gossip about me, won't cooperate with me, and try to take my job.

I need to forgive my *neighbors* for all their noise, letting their property run down, not handling their dogs who run through my property, not taking in their trashcans, being prejudiced and running down the neighborhood.

I forgive the *clergy and congregation in my Church* for their lack of support, pettiness, bad sermons, lack of friendliness, not affirming me as they should, and not providing me with inspiration, and any other hurt they may have inflicted.

I forgive all *professional* and *service people* who have hurt me in any way – doctors, nurses, lawyers, policemen, hospital workers, and any others.

I forgive my *employer* for not paying me enough for my work, for not appreciating my work, for being unkind and unreasonable, angry, unfriendly, for not promoting me when I deserved it, and for not complementing on my work.

I forgive my *schoolteachers* and *instructors* of the past as well as the present. I forgive those who punished me, humiliated me, insulted me, treated me unjustly, or called me dumb or stupid.

I forgive my *friends* who have let me down, lost contact with me, do not support me, were not available when I needed help, borrowed money and did not return it, or gossiped about me.

Heavenly Father, I especially pray for the grace of forgiveness for that *one person in life who has hurt me the most*. I ask to forgive anyone who I consider to be my *greatest enemy*, the one who is hardest to forgive or the one whom I said I would never forgive.

Thank You, Father, that I am free of the evil of unforgiveness. Let Your Holy Spirit fill me with light and let every dark area of my mind be enlightened and healed.

"Bless your persecutors; bless and do not curse them."
|(Romans 12:14)

Try using this Forgiveness Prayer for an extended period of time such as seven days, nine days, a month or more. Experience proves that the Holy Spirit will reveal people to you who need to be forgiven. Praying for a person constantly is to forgive that person by an act of the will. Negative emotions may remain, but forgiveness opens the door to healing. If you have a need to forgive someone, this prayer will change your life.

Our Father Who art in heaven,
Hallowed be Thy Name.
Thy Kingdom come.
Thy will be done
On earth as it is in heaven.

Give us this day our daily bread,
And forgive us our trespasses
As we forgive those
Who trespass against us,
And lead us not into temptation,
But deliver us from evil.

(Matthew 6:9-13)

Regarding suffering consider the words of Jesus to Sister Josefa Menendez, a Spanish nun to whom He appeared:

"Do you think that anything happens without My permission? I dispose ALL things for the good of each and every soul. Though this hour seems dark to you, My power dominates it and My work will gain by it. I am your All, so do not be afraid, for you are not alone. I have not brought you here for your ruin, but from love, and because it is fitting that all this should happen."

If you need to be reconciled with someone, forgiveness in one's heart makes the suffering so much easier to bear. The Lord will help you through any difficulty. All you need do is ask.

IV

Prayers – Do They Work? Does God Listen To Me?

Chapter 1

God, Can You Hear Me?

How do you talk to God?

Does God hear me? Since God knows everything even our innermost secret thoughts, then we must conclude that He always hears us. But does He listen? Can we talk to God in different ways or do we have to use some specific formula? Talking to God is called prayer. We can talk to God in various ways. Let's examine some of them.

There is community prayer where people pray as part of a congregation or in a group. They usually pray aloud, reciting formal prayers, singing, and joyfully praising God. There are ritualistic services designed to give worship to God. There are also prayer groups where people will lay hands on another person and pray for his/her healing or needs. Jesus Himself tells us about the power of praying together, "Again I tell you, if two of you join your voices on earth to pray for anything whatever, it shall be granted you by My Father in heaven. Where two or three are gathered in My name, there I am in their midst." (Matthew 18:19-20)

There is also private prayer. Some people like to pray silently concentrating on their petitions to God. Some like to sit quietly in a place of worship such as a church, in their room at home, in a lovely garden or other place close to nature and just put themselves in God's presence without saying anything. Others like to meditate concentrating on a specific aspect of their faith. There are many prayer books containing prayers for specific petitions and praises. And some people like to use the power of their imagination when they pray. How do you do that? You simply picture yourself in a particular situation with the Lord. For example, you might picture yourself walking and talking with God in a beautiful garden. If you are a Christian, you might picture yourself talking with Jesus about some concern in your life and imagine Him explaining to you how you can best handle the situation. Do you have to kneel when praying? We can pray kneeling, standing, sitting, or even lying down. We can use any words with which we are most comfortable. If you are angry about something, you can yell and scream, you can even complain or argue with the Lord. He doesn't mind. The most important aspect of prayer is the sincerity of your heart.

Does God answer *all* prayers?

Good question! Yes, He really does answer all prayers. Sometimes God says, "Yes" and answers your prayers right away. Sometimes you may have to wait a while, sometimes for years before you get your answer. Does that mean that God is not really listening to you unless you badger Him for a long time, and He gets tired of listening to you? Or does it mean that He doesn't really care? Actually, God cares very much. You might not believe that right now because you may have been praying for something for some time and nothing seem to be happening.

Consider this – God does what is best for each person and for his/her immortal soul. He answers prayers at just the right time; He is never late. "Ask and you will receive. Seek and you will find. Knock and it will be opened to you. For the one who asks, receives. The one who seeks, finds. The one who knocks, enters. Would one of you hand his son a stone when he asks for a loaf. . .If you, with all your sins, know how to give your children what is good, how much more will your heavenly Father give good things to anyone who asks Him!" (Matthew 7:7-11) God really and truly wants to give good things to all His children, but what you are asking for may not be what is best at the time. So, you might have to wait until the time is right for you.

Is this what we call perseverance?

If you will remember from Section II, Chapter 2, Monica prayed for her son, Augustine for something like twenty years. She shed many tears and even begged the bishop to speak to him. The bishop replied, "Go, continue to do as you do. It is impossible that a child of such tears shall perish."[54] Not only were Monica's prayers answered for the conversion of her son, but both she and her son became great saints.

Wow! I said to myself, "If God can take a stubborn, hardened sinner like Augustine and turn him into a great saint, Doctor of the Church no less, surely He can do something with a little nothing like me." Don't you agree? So, if you have been praying for something for some time and it seems that God is not paying attention, don't give up. (Satan would love that.) God *hears* and *always* answers sincere prayers at just the right time.

---

54 *Little Lives of the Great Saints*, John O'Kane Murray, pp. 196-197

Does God sometimes say, "No"?

God says, "No" when what we ask for may be detrimental to our wellbeing or lead to the loss of our soul. Check out this example:

King Louis XI of France, who became the most powerful monarch in the world, in March 1480 suffered a stroke that paralyzed him and affected his speech. Searching desperately for a cure, he brought in the leading physicians and miracle workers of Europe. No one was able to help him. Finally, he heard of the miraculous cures of Francis of Paola from Calabria, Italy. He had St. Francis brought to him. When St. Francis met with the King, he knew immediately "that whatever miracle he might have effected that would save the King physically would have condemned his soul to eternal punishment."[55]

St. Francis prayed to the Holy Spirit for guidance. He prayed with the King and counseled him. The King tried many ways to convince St. Francis to procure a healing for him. Nothing worked. The King finally became convinced of the unquestionable holiness of this man who refused silver and gold, who was most sincere and completely committed to God. He resolved to die as a good Christian, praying and listening to St. Francis. He "...died the death of a good Christian, which he had not been during the height of his power."[56]

So you see, when God says "No" it is always for a good reason. God knows all, sees all, and always does what is best. "For My thoughts are not your thoughts, nor are your ways My ways, says the Lord. As high as the heavens are above the earth, so high are My ways above your ways, and My thoughts above your thoughts." (Isaiah 55:8-9)

---

[55] *St. Francis of Paola,* Simi & Segreti, p. 135
[56] *St. Francis of Paola,* Simi & Segreti, p. 153

How often should we pray?

Should we pray once a day, once a week, whenever we go to prayer services? St. Paul says, "Rejoice always, never cease praying, render constant thanks, such is God's will for you in Christ Jesus." (Thessalonians 5:16-18) Never cease praying? Are you kidding? With our busy schedules and all our responsibilities who has time to pray constantly? Let's get real. Some of us don't even have a minute to ourselves, let alone have time to pray all day. It's not as hard as one might think. In fact it's rather easy. We can make our whole day and night a prayer. How? In the morning when you awake, just tell God that everything you do this day is all for Him, and when you go to bed at night, put all your slumber in His care. There you go – all 24 hours are covered.

Throughout the day lift your heart and mind to God. Thank Him for everything – a beautiful sunny day, the rain that makes the flowers grow and gives us fresh water to drink. Thank God for each member of your family, for your friends, even for that particular person that drives you crazy. Learn to thank God for everything that happens in your life, the good, the bad, the ugly, and the indifferent. That doesn't seem to make much sense, does it? But remember that God can turn a bad experience into something positive. Trust Him. He always takes something good out of the worst situations. You will become a much happier person because of it. You don't believe me? OK don't take my word for it. Try it for yourself for about thirty days and see what happens. Does it seem to be going rather s-l-o-w-l-y? That's OK, too. Keep it up. It will pay great dividends as time goes on.

Is there anyone sick?

"Is there anyone sick among you? He should ask for the presbyters of the Church. They in turn are to pray over him, anointing him in the Name (of the Lord). This prayer uttered in faith will reclaim the one who is ill and restore him to health." (James 5:14-16)

Did you ever pray for someone who was sick? Most people have. But did you ever pray *with* someone for healing? Does it work? Was the person healed? It's usually done by laying on of hands, perhaps anointing him/her with holy oil, and praying for healing.

A number of scientific studies have been conducted to determine whether faith and prayer really do have an effect on illness. "Studies show that religious folks who attend church regularly and practice what they believe have lower blood pressure, lower cancer rates, are less likely to be addicted to alcohol or drugs, are more likely to survive major surgery, are less likely to experience depression or commit suicide, are better able to cope with chronic disease, and live longer. Even more amazing, in certain cases, lack of religious belief has been found to be as bad for our health as smoking and drinking."[57]

Does praying for healing really work?

"A study was done at San Francisco General Hospital between 1982 and 1983 involving 393 cardiac patients who were divided into two groups. . .one group was prayed for (without them knowing about it). . .Patients in the other group were not prayed for. No one in the study knew which patients were being prayed for. The only people who knew were the Christians (doing the praying) who only knew the patient's first name, diagnosis, general condition, and a request to pray for a rapid recovery and freedom from complications. Those patients who had received intercessory prayer had less congestive heart failure, needed less antibiotics, had fewer episodes of pneumonia, had fewer

---

[57] *Prayer, Faith and Healing,* By Kenneth Winston Caine and Brian Paul Kaufman, p. 4

cardiac arrests. . .the results were startling enough to spawn a wealth of studies on prayer research."[58]

Did you ever pray with someone or have someone pray with you for healing? I did, and I would like to share some of my experiences with you. I have been doing this for many years and have had some amazing things happen.

When my older son, Eric was in fourth grade, he had a problem with his stomach. A number of times I had to run up to the school to pick him up. One night at our prayer group meeting, I asked for prayers for him. One of our members said to me, "Pat, don't pray for him, pray with him." I did pray with Eric, and he never had that problem again.

Many years ago, one evening in August, my husband's cousin came over our house with his wife, Carol, and her little six-year old daughter. Little Mary had broken her arm which was in a cast. My daughter, Rosemary, about the same age, wanted to play with Mary, but her mother would not want her to do anything. She explained that Mary's arm was not healing properly and it would have to be re-broken and reset. The poor little girl and her mother were so scared. I asked Carol if she was familiar with healing prayer. She wasn't very religious and knew nothing about healing prayer. I explained it to her and asked if we could pray with Mary. I said the worst that could happen is nothing; the best thing is that her arm would be healed. She agreed, so I called my three children, Eric, Christopher, and Rosemary. We placed our hands on Mary, I anointed her with some holy oil, and we prayed for her to be healed. I gave Carol some holy oil and told her to pray with Mary every day for healing. I don't know whether or not she did. Sometime in October, I happened to talk to her again and asked how Mary's arm was. She said it was the same. I told her

---

58   Ibid, pp. 5-7

not to give up because sometimes the Lord heals slowly. It wasn't until January that something was telling me to call her and find out how Mary's arm was. She said to me, "You won't believe this. The doctor was amazed. Her arm is completely healed and did not have to be re-broken." I had only one thing to say, "Praise the Lord!"

When Mike was 16 years old, he was in an auto accident, and as a result injured his spinal cord which left him paralyzed from the waist down. Being a Eucharistic Minister, I began bringing Holy Communion to Mike and to pray with him for healing. He had gone through a difficult depressing time knowing he would never walk again. Now remember that God always does what is best for the person. Was Mike healed and able to walk again? No, he received a different kind of healing. Mike had been very athletic, playing football, etc. All this was gone when his accident occurred. Or was it? Mike entered the Special Olympics and won a number of medals in wheelchair races. He was such an inspiration to others who suffered from similar circumstances. He continued his education, graduating from college with a degree in Accounting. All that he accomplished was amazing. Mike is married, has a great job, and owns his own home. And Mike is happy. Not all healings are physical.

Do you have to be there?

Does one have to be present and lay hands on a person in order to affect a healing? A number of years ago, on a Monday, Rosie came to me and said, "Pray for my son, Jerry. He has a terrible fear of the dark." I assured her that I would pray for Jerry. I knew how terrifying a fear of the dark could be because I had suffered from it well into my thirties when it finally left me. On Tuesday morning I went to daily Mass and Communion as is my custom. When I came home, I sat on my couch. Since it was about 9 o'clock, I figured that Jerry must be in school. I closed my eyes and pictured Jerry sitting at his desk. Then I pictured Jesus walking up to him and laying His hands on Jerry and healing him of his fear of the dark. Later that week, Friday to be exact, I saw Rosie again. She came up to me and said, "Praise God! Jerry isn't afraid of the dark anymore." I said, "That's wonderful! When did this happen?" She said, "On Tuesday."

God can do anything. He is not restricted by time or space. Faith and prayer can change the outcome of any situation. Don't be afraid to make use of it.

I am so glad I have a loving Father God Who always looks out for me, aren't you? It makes a lot of sense to always put all your trust in God. He will never steer you wrong. Where else could you be assured of the very best outcome for you as a result of your asking, of your prayers? Believe It! It is really true even though you may not see it immediately or even in this life. You will definitely see it in the next, and that time is not so far away as one may think. This life is very short, even if one lives to reach 100 years old. Think about it. The next phase of your life lasts for an eternity. Don't you want to spend it in heaven with God and all the wonderful angels, saints, family members and friends – all beauty and happiness forever? I sure do! All you have to do is ask God for it with a sincere heart.

CHAPTER 2

Some Misconceptions?

What madness is this?

In our country, the United States of America, according to our Constitution, we have the right to worship or not to worship God or any god as we so choose. But do some people use prayer to try to manipulate God? Do they use religion as an excuse in order to advance their own agendas?

Take a look at the terrorist group ISIS and the jihadists. These terrorists murder innocent people in the name of religion. They are taught from the time they are children that if they kill a Jew or Christian, they will go straight to heaven. What kind of madness is this? What kind of god would advocate the murder of innocent people? This sounds like a god that does not exist except in the minds of perverse people. Good Muslim people don't want this terrorism. They want peace, prosperity, and safety so that they can have a good living for themselves and for their children just like the rest of us.

Those who use violence to try to achieve their own goals must be following an evil source. Could this evil source be Satan himself? If that is true, then all these evildoers will eventually come to a bad end because that's what Satan wants – the destruction of humankind. Go back to Section II of this book, Chapter 3. Read again about Hell starting on page 99. This is what Satan wants. Is this what humankind wants also? I doubt it. God wants us to love each other as brothers and sisters, not to kill each other. God wants us to have peace, prosperity, and a good life right here on earth. He is the Creator of all people, a loving God, not one of violence and destruction.

Do we sometimes try to manipulate God? Many of us do, maybe without realizing it. We try to bargain with God. We promise to do a certain thing in return for a particular favor that we want from God. Have you done this? I know I have. Realize this, you cannot manipulate God. He will do whatever is best for you regardless of how you try to convince Him otherwise.

Are Mary and the Saints sometimes worshipped?

Worship is given to God alone. Catholic Christians do not worship Mary, the mother of Jesus. This is a popular misconception among some denominations of Christians. Mary is honored, not worshipped by Catholics. The saints are likewise honored because of the exemplary lives they led while on earth. When a prayer is said to Mary or a particular saint, it is for the purpose of asking for his/her intercession with God for a particular grace or favor. Since Mary and the saints are much closer to God, they are in a better position to obtain our requests than we are. Some people prefer to go straight to Jesus, God the Father, or the Holy Spirit. Whichever way you choose to pray is fine. The important thing is not what you say, how you say it, how many prayers you say, or how long you pray, but rather the sincerity of your heart.

Some Misconceptions?

Is the Rosary a prayer in worship of Mary?

Again, Mary is not worshipped. The Rosary is a series of meditations on the life of Jesus. The Joyful Mysteries concentrate on the early life of Jesus. The Sorrowful Mysteries depict His passion and death on the cross. The Luminous Mysteries remind us of some of the important events in Jesus' life. The Glorious Mysteries deal with His resurrection and ascension into heaven, the coming of the Holy Spirit, the assumption of Mary into heaven, and her coronation as Queen of the Universe. As Mary is the mother of Jesus, these great honors were conferred upon her. Wouldn't you want to honor your mother? Jesus did. There is also the Scriptural Rosary which is essentially the same, however, it goes into more detail by using Scripture passages from the New Testament dealing with these same aspects of Jesus' life.

How powerful is the Rosary?

Remember in 1978 when Ted Bundy killed all those girls except one. The terrified girl had refused to talk to anyone except a priest. She then told Father Kerr that before she went off to college, her mother made her promise to say the Rosary every night for her protection. That night when Ted Bundy came into her room with murder in mind, the Rosary was in her hand. He never touched her because a strong force was preventing him from going any further. He dropped his weapon and ran.[59]

How about this for the power of the Rosary?

Year: 1945. Place: Hiroshima, Japan. Event: Dropping the Bomb. Result: Total destruction. An estimated 140,000 people were killed. Many suffered horrible disfigurement from radiation burns and illness from radiation poisoning. Everyone within one mile of the bomb

---

59   "Rosary stopped Ted Bundy," snopes.com

explosion died. **Or did they?** There was a small community of Jesuit Catholic priests and brothers living eight blocks from the center of the blast. Among them was Father Hubert Schiffer, S.J., 30 years old at the time. Hearing the sound of the blast, upon opening the door, they were utterly astounded and dumbfounded to find nothing standing except the house in which they resided. All 16 members were spared. They were not even affected by the radiation. Father lived 33 more years in good health. In 1976 in Philadelphia, PA he related his story. More than 200 doctors and scientists examined and questioned him. They were unable to explain how these 16 men survived when everyone else around them were dead. The rectory (priests' dwelling) which is still standing today, was thoroughly investigated and examined throughout the years. It could not be determined as to why it remained untouched by the devastation. Father Schiffer explained the difference – ". . .in that house the Rosary was said each day."[60]

Does the Rosary work? You better believe it. Just ask someone who knows.

What is a novena?

Novena means nine. This is a prayer or prayers that are said for nine days usually as a petition asking for a particular grace or favor. Other "novenas" may be said on a weekly basis, for thirty days, or however long one desires to pray for the grace or favor. It could be a novena to God, Jesus, or the Holy Spirit, or to honor Mary or a particular saint asking for their intercession for the desired favor.

---

60   Msgr. Nicholas I Puhak, St. Mary's Byzantine Catholic Church, *Hazleton Standard-Speaker,* August 14, 2010, p. A15

What types of prayer are there?

The prayer of **petition** asks for something from God. All good things come from God. The prayer of **praise** gives worship to God for all His marvelous creations and for everything in our lives. This usually goes along with the prayer of **thanksgiving** for all that He does for us. Everything we have, every good thing that we do all comes from God. The prayer of **contrition** tells God that we are sorry for having offended him.

Prayers do not have to be long. They can be short **ejaculations** such as: My God, I love You! My Jesus mercy! Thank You, Lord, for Your goodness! It can be whatever short message you wish to convey to God. Again, the most important aspect of any prayer is the sincere intention of your heart.

Do some people worship statues?

Worshipping statues would be idolatry and is specifically forbidden by God in the first commandment, "I, the Lord, am your God,. . .You shall not have other gods besides Me. You shall not carve idols for yourselves. . .you shall not bow down before them or worship them. . ." (Exodus 20:2-5) Some Christians believe that Catholic Christians worship statues. This is a false premise. Why then do Catholics have statues in their churches and their homes? Statues and other articles blessed by the priest are called sacramentals. Their purpose is to remind us of God, Jesus, Mary, a particular saint, much like having photos of your mother, father, family members, friends, or of a particular event. Medals are not to be carried as a superstitious article such as a lucky rabbit's foot. The medal in itself has no power. All power comes from God. The medal is a reminder of God or of a particular saint and to invoke his/her intercession in prayer. You can also ask members of your family or friends whom the Lord has called into eternity to pray for you as well. It is wonderful to know that we have this connection with those who have gone before us and are in God's company. This is called the Communion of Saints.

Whose is better?

There is one more aspect of misunderstanding that should be mentioned – some people think that their religion is better than that of someone else's beliefs. For example, is one Christian religion better than that of another denomination? Is there one that is better than all the rest or are we all basically the same and it doesn't matter which one you follow? The Christian religions are very similar. There are, however, some major differences – too much to go into a lengthy discussion here. If you have some doubts about your faith, do some investigating to see whether or not you agree with what you have learned. You may find that your belief system is perfectly fine for you. Or you may find that something is missing and you may find what you are looking for elsewhere.

Caution: Don't change your belief system because you don't like what your pastor, minister, priest, or rabbi happened to say. Perhaps it hit a nerve because you are not following God's laws and living accordingly. Don't lie to yourself saying that what you are doing is alright if it really isn't. Of course, you can't lie to God because He *knows* all. And don't change because you want to please someone else, such as a boyfriend, new spouse, employer, someone pressuring you to join his/her group. The change must come from your own heart because you feel that it would bring you closer to God. There are many paths to God. You need to embrace the one that is right for you. Ask the Holy Spirit to guide you. He is always there to help you, will never steer you wrong.

Who was Jewish?

Judaism is actually the root of Christianity. After all, Jesus was a Jew as was His Mother Mary, His foster father Joseph, and all of His disciples. Jesus followed all the Jewish traditions and the law. He said, "Do not think that I have come to abolish the law and the prophets. I have come not to abolish them, but to fulfill them. Of this much I assure you: until heaven and earth pass away, not the smallest letter of the law, not the smallest part of a letter, shall be done away with until it all comes true." (Matthew 5:17-18)

Jesus is the long-awaited Messiah of the Old Testament. Do you have any doubts about this? Read it for yourself. Pay special attention to Isaiah who describes what the Messiah will accomplish when He comes. (Isaiah 42:1-9, 52:13-15, 53:1-12) There are also other passages in the Old Testament that refer to the Messiah. Now read the Gospels of Matthew, Mark, Luke, and John. Does it take too long to read all these Gospels? Why not buy or rent the movie, *Jesus of Nazareth*, which gives an excellent depiction of the life of Jesus Christ – what He taught, His miracles, and His redemptive suffering and death on the cross for our sins that we may have everlasting life. Through reading the Old Testament and the Gospels you will probably come to one conclusion – Jesus Christ *is* the long-awaited Messiah.

The Jews, at the time of Jesus, for the most part, rejected Jesus as the Messiah. Many of the Jews of today are still waiting for the Messiah to come. Consider this: Almost all of the followers of Jesus were Jews. They really believed in Him and put their lives on the line for Him and His teachings. All but one of His apostles, John, were martyred. Many of the early Christians were tortured and put to death because of their faith. Now ask yourself, would all of these people die for a lie? Many Christians even today are persecuted and some put to death for their faith in some parts of the world. Would they die for a lie? Not likely. Jews are also persecuted. Christians believe that Jesus will come again. For them it will be the second coming of the Messiah, as Jesus promised. For those Jews who are still waiting, will it be the first coming of the Messiah? Where do you stand on this?

What about all those who don't believe in Judaism or Christianity?

What about the Muslims, the Hindus, those who worship Buddha, those who believe in other so-called pagan religions? What happens to them? My Mom always said, "There are good and bad in all kinds of people." Remember that each person is made in the image and likeness of God, and God loves *each one* of His children. Does that mean those who don't believe in Him, those who never even heard of God or of His Son, Jesus? Will these people be deprived of salvation through no fault of their own? Would a good and loving God turn them away? Blessed Anne Catherine Emmerich, the Augustinian nun and visionary who bore the stigmata (wounds of Jesus) said, "I had the happy assurance that no soul was lost whom ignorance alone hindered from knowing Jesus, who had a vague desire to know Him (God), and who had not lived in the state of grievous sin."[61] This means that people who have not known Jesus or God, but who are loving and desire to do the right things, treating others with respect, are welcome in God's kingdom. Will God give them some kind of choice to accept Him or reject Him when they die? Only God knows the answer to that. But since God is so good, so loving, and desires the salvation of all His children, it seems reasonable that He will be most congenial to these people. Doesn't that make sense to you?

---

61   *The Life of Anne Catherine Emmerich,* Carl E. Schmoger, C.SS.R., p. 546

How does God handle people who do not know Him?

According to Joel C. Rosenberg, author of a number of best-selling books, in his book *Inside the Revolution*, in 1979 there were about 500 Muslim converts to Christianity in Iran. However, between 2000 and 2008 the number of converts increased unbelievably. An Iranian director of one of the largest evangelization ministries stated that he believes the *number* of converts to Christianity is close to seven million, about one in every ten in Iran. In Egypt there are more than 2.5 million Christians with more and more conversions taking place. In 2008 in Iraq, several million Arabic New Testament Bibles and Christian books were sent. Millions are being printed inside the country, and they are having difficulty keeping up with the demand. Islamic clerics have become so alarmed by all the conversions that in 2006 Algerian officials passed a law banning Muslims from becoming Christians or even learning about Christianity. Why so many converts? One Sudanese Christian leader said, "People see what radical Islam is like and they want Jesus instead."[62]

Radical Islam promotes persecution, degradation of women, genocide, suicide bombers, entices children to walk mine fields to blow themselves up promising them paradise. This was done in Iran so that soldiers could move easily through mined areas to fight enemies. What kind of religion promotes such destruction of life? It is no wonder that so many Muslims are turning to Christianity where they find love, forgiveness, and a self-worth knowing that the God of the Universe loves each and every one of His children; God loves *them*.

---

62   *Inside The Revolution*, Joel C. Rosenberg, p. 381 f.

Is there any danger in becoming a Christian? Absolutely. "Once they make a decision to follow Christ. . .believers face the threat of persecution, torture, and death from neighbors, and sometimes their governments. . .They also face ostracism from family members and friends."[63] These people have to keep their Christian faith secret in order not to be put to death even by their own family members. Many have fled the country of their birth in order to escape with their lives. If you were in their shoes, what would you do?

Why is God in the person of Jesus reaching out to Muslims?

The answer is simple – God loves *all* His children. He wants all to be saved, to be happy with Him for all eternity. How is He doing this? Through miracles. Miracles? That's right, miracles. Incredible miracles have been taking place in Muslim countries. God is healing Muslims of sickness and diseases. People are seeing visions of Jesus Who is speaking to them of love and forgiveness, and they are repenting of their sins, reforming their lives, and following Jesus the Savior. Read the true story of Mina Nevisa in her book *Miracle of Miracles*, an Iranian woman born into a family of Islamic fundamentalists. Her account of her harrowing experiences trying to escape torture and death, leaving Iran, traveling through danger-ridden countries before finally making it to freedom in the United States. You can get it on Amazon.com.

Wouldn't you want to know the truth?

Why is all this happening? Jesus said, ". . .then you will know the truth and the truth will set you free." (John 8:32) What did Jesus mean? He tells us, "I give you my assurance, everyone who lives in

---

63   Ibid, p. 375

sin is the slave of sin." (John 8:34) What is sin? Sin is going against God's commandments to love God above all else and to love your neighbor as yourself.

Right now the question is: Do you want to know the truth? If the answer is "yes," then come along. Jesus said, "I am the way, the truth, and the life; no one comes to the Father but through Me." (John 14:6) If Jesus is the *truth* and no one comes to the Father but through Him, then doesn't it make sense to follow Him? On the other hand, if you are still skeptical, but curious, come along and see. If you really don't care one way or the other, come along anyway just to see what happens. If your answer is "no," come along, too. You have nothing to lose by doing so. You, too are most welcome.

Whatever your position, why not say this little prayer? It is non-denominational. If you are an atheist, say it anyway even if you don't believe it and it is only words to you. Be open to the truth whatever that is just because you would really like to know what is *really the truth*. Let the Holy Spirit lead you. Even if you don't believe that there is a Holy Spirit, **be open**. You may be surprised as to how things will turn out for you. All you need is a sincere heart and God will do the rest.

> **O, Lord God the Most High, Creator of the Universe, I want to know the truth. If You truly are, then help me to know it. Open my eyes that I may see the truth. Open my mind that I may know and understand the truth. Open my heart that I may embrace the truth. Help me to know that You truly love *me*. Help me to know what You desire of me that I may find happiness with You for all eternity.**
>
> **Amen.**

Prayer To The Great Spirit

O' Great Spirit, Whose voice I hear in the winds;
Whose breath gives life to all the world, hear me!
I am small and weak, I need your strength,
I need Your wisdom.
Let me walk in Beauty, and make my eyes ever
Behold the red and purple sunset.
Make my hands respect the things You have made
And my ears sharp to hear Your voice.
Make me wise so that I may understand
The things You have taught my people.
Let me learn the lessons you have hidden
In every leaf and rock.
I seek strength, not to be greater than my brother,
But to fight my greatest enemy – myself.
Make me always ready to come to you
With clean hands and straight eyes.
So when life fades, as the fading sunset,
My spirit may come to You without shame.

Footsteps of Wisdom, To educate the heart as well as the mind is our sacred trust.
Red Cloud Indian School
South Dakota

V

**Miracles!
Miracles – Really?**

Chapter 1

Do You Believe In Miracles?

What is a miracle?

Webster's Dictionary defines a "miracle" as an effect or extraordinary event in the physical world which surpasses all known human or natural powers and is ascribed to a supernatural cause. To put it more simply, a miracle is a physical event that takes place for which there is no natural explanation; it is usually considered as an act or work of God. Do miracles really happen? Actually, supernatural miracles have been taking place for thousands of years and even happen in modern times.

Would you like some examples?

In the Old Testament King Nebuchadnezzar of Babylon tried to force three Jews, Shadrach, Meshach, and Abednego to worship a golden statue. They refused to do so putting their trust in God. When the king threatened to throw them into the fiery furnace, they replied, "There is no need for us to defend ourselves before you in this matter. If our God, whom we serve, can save us from the white-hot furnace, O king, may He save us! But even if He will not, know, O king, that we will not serve your god or worship the golden statue which you set up." (Daniel 3:16-18)

The king became very angry and had them thrown into the white-hot furnace after having it heated seven times hotter. They walked about in the flames and a fourth person was walking around with them. The king was astonished to hear them singing and seeing them alive. He called them out of the fire. When the three came out, there was no evidence of fire about them. (The fourth was probably an angel.) King Nebuchadnezzar exclaimed, "Blessed be the God of Shadrach, Meshach, and Abednego who sent His angel to deliver the servants that trusted in Him. . ." (Daniel 3:95) The three were saved; the king believed and ordered his subjects to respect their God. Read the entire account in the book of Daniel, Chapter 3. That's what I call some kind of miracle, don't you?

How about another Old Testament example?

Naaman was a commander in the army of the king of Aram and he was a leper. A little girl from Israel was a servant of his wife. The little girl told her mistress that Naaman should go to the prophet in Samaria. Naaman went to Elisha, the man of God, who told him to go and wash seven times in the Jordan river. Naaman was angry and said that he could have washed in the rivers of Damascus. His servants reasoned with him to do as the prophet had said. Reluctantly Naaman went and washed seven times in the Jordan. His flesh became again like that of a child. He was cured of his leprosy. (2 Kings 5:1-15) Another amazing miracle! How wonderful is that?!!

Who is the god you worship?

All this power comes from God. Can your god perform miracles? Only a true God can do the seemingly impossible. What about Jesus? He performed some incredible miracles. He must be God; doesn't that make sense? We know about His miracles of healing many people of their illnesses. Some people might say that because they believed that He could heal them, they were healed. It was a psychological happening. Our minds can do marvelous things. OK, if that's what you think. So let's look at some miracles that do not have a human element in them.

Jesus and His disciples got into a boat. Jesus fell asleep. Suddenly a violent storm came up on the lake. The disciples were frightened and woke Jesus saying, "Lord, save us!. . .He said to them, 'Where is your courage? How little faith you have!' Then He stood up and took the wind and the sea to task. Complete calm ensued; the men were dumbfounded. "What sort of man is this. . .that even the winds and sea obey Him?" (Matthew 8:25-27) What sort of man is this? Who else could command the winds and the sea? He must be God. If you are not a Christian, could your god do that? Maybe you might want to check out this Jesus guy Who *could* command the wind and sea. It may be well worth looking into.

How did He do that?

On another occasion, Jesus had His disciples get into a boat without Him. He then went to the mountain to pray. When evening came, the boat was far out on the lake. Jesus "came walking toward them on the water. . .When they saw Him walking on the lake, they thought it was a ghost and began to cry out. They had all seen Him and were terrified. He hastened to reassure them: 'Get hold of yourselves! It is I. Do not be afraid!' He got into the boat with them and the wind died down. They were taken aback by these happenings. . ." (Mark 6:48-51) Did you ever try walking on water? It isn't too easy, is it?

What was Jesus' greatest miracle?

Jesus was arrested and condemned to the shameful death of a criminal – death by crucifixion even though He was innocent of any crime. He was scourged mercilessly, a crown of thorns embedded into His head, mocked and ridiculed, made to carry His own cross, then crucified, died and was buried. On the third day after His death, He rose from the dead in a glorified body. He appeared to His disciples. "On the evening of the first day of the week, even though the disciples had locked the doors of the place where they were for fear of the Jews, Jesus came and stood before them. 'Peace be with you,' He said. . .He showed them His hands and His side. At the sight of the Lord, the disciples rejoiced." (John 20:19-20) "In their panic and fright they thought they were seeing a ghost. He said to them. . .'Look at My hands and My feet; it is really I. Touch Me, and see that a ghost does not have flesh and bones as I do.'. .They gave Him a piece of cooked fish which He took and ate in their presence." (Luke 24:37, 39, 42-43)

Jesus appeared to His disciples a number of times over the next forty days. "Then He led them out near Bethany, and with His hands upraised, blessed them. . .and was taken up into heaven. They returned to Jerusalem filled with joy." (Luke 24:50-52) All this is definitely true. How do we know? These disciples were eye witnesses to these events. They put their lives on the line and were killed for their beliefs. How many people would die for a lie? I certainly would not die for a lie. Would you?

What is the Shroud of Turin?

The Shroud of Turin is believed to be the burial cloth of Jesus. There is some powerful and overwhelming evidence that indicates not only that it is real but points to the occurrence of a supernatural event after

His death. Recent analyses of the Shroud using modern scientific equipment reveal amazing information. Scientific studies confirm that the Shroud is the burial cloth of a crucified Jewish man who died at the hands of the Romans. Forensic evidence shows that this man's death was not only consistent with the unique characteristics of the Gospel accounts of Matthew, Mark, Luke, and John as to His scourging and crucifixion, but that the death took place about the time of Passover in the area of the city of Jerusalem.

In 1978 a team of experts was given permission to examine the Shroud. The Shroud of Turin Research Project (STURP) study group included 35 top scientists, physicists, chemists, NASA image specialists, electrical engineers, a forensic pathologist and others. In 1981 they issued a stunning and unanimous report: "We can conclude that the Shroud image is that of a real human form of a scourged, crucified man. It is not the product of an artist. The bloodstains are composed of hemoglobin and also give a positive test for serum albumin." A number of key findings about the image have been made by STURP and other studies:

> It was not painted; no pigment was found.

> It is a two-dimensional image with encoded three-dimensional information.

> The distance between body and cloth is captured in the density of the image; closer is darker.

> The image did not come from contact with the cloth.

> The image appears to be created by an oscillating strobe of high intensity light with a simple wave length.

The light came from inside the body.

The event happened in 1/40th of a billionth of a second like a laser beam, moving 2.5 billion watts.

To create a similar light one would need all the electric power generated on Earth.

Dr. Paolo Di Lazzaro, lead author on the report, STURP ENEA Research Centre found that the Shroud of Turin is not a fake, and the body image was formed by a sort of electromagnetic source of energy.[64] The complete article regarding the Shroud of Turin can be found in NEWSMAX, April 2023, pages 46 to 52 inclusive. You can also check out Newsmax.com.[65]

The report said that the **light came from inside the body.** This means that *Jesus raised Himself from the dead.* "The Father loves Me for this: that I lay down My life to take it up again. No one takes it from Me; I lay it down freely. I have power to lay it down and I have power to take it up again. This command I received from My Father." (John 10:17-18) Jesus is God. He has the power to raise Himself from the dead.

---

64   Newsmax, April 2023, pp. 46, 48, 49, 52
65   Ibid, pp. 46-52

CHAPTER 2

Do Miracles Still Happen?

Do miracles happen in this day and age?

Jesus' miracles happened 2000 years ago. Fast forward to the year 1917, to Fatima, Portugal where there was a miracle that was witnessed by approximately 70,000 people. That's right, 70,000 people. What happened that was so spectacular?

Three children had visions of the Blessed Virgin Mary who appeared for six consecutive months on the 13th day of the month beginning in May. The Blessed Virgin had a special message for the world. She showed them a terrifying vision of hell. She said that God wished to establish devotion to her Immaculate Heart and to say the Rosary. If this was done, then many souls would be saved and there would be peace. (This was at the time of World War I) If people did not stop offending God, another worse war would ensue; hence, World War II.

In July the Blessed Virgin Mary promised a miracle that would take place on her last visit so that all people would believe. As promised, on October 13 the miracle known as the "Miracle of the Sun" took place. A large crowd of about 70,000 people, including newspaper reporters and photographers, had gathered. Heavy rains poured down for some time, then finally stopped leaving everything very wet and muddy. One of the children, Lucia, pointed to the sun. People were able to look at it without discomfort to their eyes. The sun began to spin and change colors, then appeared to fall from the sky toward the earth radiating heat. When it returned to the sky, everything was dry including the mud. This miracle was witnessed up to thirty miles away.

Did you ever witness a miracle?

There are many miracles that have taken place and are still taking place today. Did you happen to see something that happened for which there is no explanation? My own experiences have left me believing the unimaginable.

As a Eucharistic Minister, I take Holy Communion to people who are sick and cannot get to church. One Tuesday I decided to take Communion to someone. Usually I call first, but for some reason, I did not call that day. Anyway, when I got to his house, he was not home, so I brought the Holy Eucharist with me to my house. I am supposed to either take It back to the church or to consume It myself. I did not consume It immediately and instead put It in my bedroom. I intended to consume It a little later when I would take time to pray. In the meantime, my sister Jean, called me and asked me to pray for Jimmy. He had been diagnosed with cancer and was to go to Hershey Medical Center on Thursday for surgery. She said that he was devastated and felt that he would not survive the surgery – he felt that he was doing to die. I told her that I was willing to pray with him, and he was welcome to come to my house.

He, along with my sister, did come to my house. As soon as he walked in the door he said, "I can only stay a half hour." He ended up staying three hours. We sat down in my living room, and I asked Jimmy and Jean to put their hands on my head and to pray to the Holy Spirit to give me the words that He wanted Jimmy to hear. After we prayed, I asked Jimmy to tell me something about himself. At 32 years of age he had a lot of health problems. He was Catholic but had been away from his faith for some time. I went to my bedroom and brought my pix which held the Holy Eucharist and showed it to him. I explained how good Jesus is and told him about miracles that have taken place through Jesus in the Holy Eucharist. I further told him that he needed to go to confession and receive Jesus again. I explained that I could not give him Communion because I am not a priest and could not hear his confession. I asked if he wanted me to pray with him for healing to which he replied, "Yes." I explained that Jesus, being God, could do anything from giving him a feeling of peace to giving him a complete healing and to know that God would do what is best for him. I told Jimmy that I did not know what Jesus would do. I placed the pix in his hands and placed my hands on his head and prayed. I have no idea what I said, and after I finished, Jimmy said, "I am completely healed, I don't have cancer any more." I was stunned, and didn't know what to say. I didn't want to give Jimmy any false hopes so I said, "I don't know. I have no way of knowing what took place. I don't know what kind of healing you may have received." But Jimmy insisted that he was healed. He was still going to Hershey on Thursday. I told him to come back and let me know how he was doing. He said that he would.

Two days later, my sister called me and said, "You are not going to believe this." I asked, "What happened?" She told me that Jimmy went down to Hershey, but he would not let the doctor do the surgery. Instead, he insisted that they do the tests all over again and in doing so, they found no sign of cancer. I must confess that I was utterly amazed. Jimmy never did come back to see me nor did I ever talk with him again. About six years later, Jimmy died. I don't know if his cancer returned or if he died from other causes. Perhaps God gave him six more years as a way for him to return to his faith and work out his salvation, I don't know. What I do know is that God is so good like that. God gives us every opportunity and every grace because He wants each and every one of us to be happy with Him in heaven eternally.

Would you like another example?

Eileen George who had a healing ministry was giving a three-day retreat. Some friends of mine were in attendance and they related to me this account of a particular healing to which they were eye witnesses. Two seats in front of them was a man who had been on this retreat. On the final evening there was a healing service to which his wife came with her baby of about 18 months old. The baby had a heart problem and was in need of surgery to correct it. My friends described the baby as listless and as having an ashen colored complexion. His little head was tilted to one side resting on his mother's shoulder in a tired-like posture. Eileen who was in front of the group was praying. She looked at the people and announced that Jesus was healing a baby. This baby suddenly picked up his little head, the color returned to his little cheeks, and he got down off his mother's lap and to the astonishment of everyone began to run around. This happened a number of years ago. He grew to be a teenager and never did have the surgery. How wonderful is this?!!

Did you ever have a miracle happen directly for you?

This happened about seven years ago. Since I was in my seventies it seemed rather prudent to be extra cautious when going down the stairs. Falling down the stairs can be disastrous at any age but especially when you are older. Therefore, I always say a little prayer when on the stairs, "Dear God, keep me safe on the stairs and keep Ron safe, too." Ron was my husband, now deceased. Ron never did fall on the stairs.

As a Eucharistic Minister it was my week to serve at daily Mass. It was on a Wednesday a week and a half before Christmas that year. Part of my duty was to take the items used as Mass and put them away in the sacristy down the stairs to the left of the altar. I picked up the chalice, paten, and purificator, put them in my left hand, and started to walk down the stairs. There are five or six steps leading to a solid wall at the bottom and a right turn into the sacristy. Somehow, I overstepped with my left foot and started to fall forward. With my right hand I quickly grabbed the railing on the right side of the steps to prevent myself from falling. Lunging forward, I banged my right elbow really hard on the two-inch thick, army green colored railing. That really hurt. Thanking God that I did not fall, I continued down the stairs thinking that I was going to have a nasty black and blue mark on my elbow. Incredibly I did not drop the chalice, paten, or purificator that were in my left hand when they should have gone crashing down hitting the wall at the bottom of the stairs.

When I got home, I checked my elbow. It was skinned and in a day or two formed two little scabs. To my amazement, however, it never did turn black and blue. The next morning I had to go down those same stairs again to put away the items used at Mass. It was then, to my utter astonishment that I realized that *there is no railing* on the right side of the stairs. How could I describe the two-inch thick army green colored railing on the right side of the stairs that is not there? I have no explanation for it. I still say my little prayer, "Dear God, keep me safe on the stairs," and "Thank You dear God for keeping me safe on the stairs."

Miracle in Hungary – He came?

On December 17, 1956, a few days before Christmas, in Communist-occupied Hungary, the faith of children prevailed. Their teacher, Miss Gertrude, a militant atheist, missed no opportunity to ridicule her Christian 10-year old students. One student, Angela, asked Father Norbert to allow her to receive Holy Communion daily to help her withstand her teacher's constant persecution. She had confidence in the strength she would receive from Jesus.

Miss Gertrude invented a cruel game to put an end to her students "ancestral superstitions." She questioned Angela, "What do you say when your parents call you?" Angela replied, "I'm coming." The teacher continued with examples of people calling for someone and getting the answer that the person is coming. The teacher said, "That's because they exist. But what if your parents call your grandmother who died, will she come?" Then she mentioned a few fairytale characters. "if you call them, they will not come because they do not exist." Then she sent Angela out of the room. She had the other student call her. Angela came in. Then the teacher said, "When you call someone, they come because they exist. When you call someone who does not exist, he does not and cannot come." Then she said, "Now suppose you call the Baby Jesus, do you think He will hear you." The students timidly replied, "Yes, we do." She asked Angela who replied, "Yes, I do." Miss Gertrude laughed and said, "let's see." She then told the children to call loudly, "Come, Child Jesus!" The girls were silent. The teacher said, "That's my point, that's my proof! You dare not call Him, because you know He will not come, your Child Jesus...because He doesn't exist." Referring to Angela, she said, "The infamous girl has been crushed!" Angela rushed to the front of the room and shouted, "Listen girls, we are going to call Him! Let's all call together: Come Infant Jesus!" They all stood up and called:

"Come Infant Jesus!" Angela said, "Again!" They shouted loudly again, "Come Infant Jesus!"

Then the extraordinary happened. The door opened silently and a great light grew and then became a globe of fire which then cracked open and in it appeared a child, a delightful child the likes of which had never been seen before. He smiled at them without uttering a word. Then He disappeared into the globe of light, and the door closed by itself. The terrified teacher screamed, "He came!" She fled down the hallway and later had to be taken to an asylum. Father Norbert questioned all the girls individually and found no contradiction in their accounts.[66]

---

66 *"He Came!"* Miracle in Hungary, Signs and Wonders for Our Times, Vol.34 No.3/4, Fall/Winter 2022

Chapter 3

What are Eucharistic Miracles?

What is the Holy Eucharistic? Are there Miracles?

The word eucharist comes from the Greek word meaning thanksgiving. When Jesus celebrated the Passover meal with His disciples, He gave thanks to God His Father in heaven. Christians know this Passover meal as the Last Supper. Exactly what did Jesus do and why is this so significant for us today?

At the beginning of the meal, Jesus washed the feet of His disciples and dried them with a towel. "He picked up a towel and tied it around Himself. Then He poured water into a basin and began to wash His disciples' feet and dry them with the towel He had around Him...He said to them, 'Do you understand what I just did for you? You address Me as Teacher and Lord, and fittingly enough, for that is what I am, but if I washed your feet – I who am Teacher and Lord – then you must wash each other's feet. What I did was to give you an example: as I have done, so you must do.'" (John 13:4-5, 12-15)

Think about it. Jesus is the Son of God, the Second Person of the Holy Trinity; Jesus is God, and He was washing our feet; He was serving us. That took a great deal of humility for the Most High God, our Creator, to come to earth and serve us. We can't even begin to imagine God's great love for us. What more could He do?

So the first thing Jesus did was to give us an example to serve others. What did it take for Jesus to do this? Hang on, there *is* more – a great deal more. The next thing Jesus did was to consecrate the bread and wine and change it into His body and blood. Does this mean that He changed it into a symbol of His body and blood? Absolutely not! Read the Scriptures. "During the meal Jesus took bread, blessed it, broke it, and gave it to His disciples. "'Take this and eat it,' He said, 'this is My body.' Then He took a cup, gave thanks, and gave it to them. 'All of you must drink from it,' He said, 'for this is My blood, the blood of the covenant, to be poured out in behalf of many for the forgiveness of sins.'" (Matthew 26:26-28) Jesus did not say, "This a symbol of My body," He said, "This *is* My body," and "This *is* My blood." So He actually changed bread and wine into His body and blood? Now that seems a little farfetched, but does it? Remember that Jesus *is God*. He can do anything. Is it too hard for God to change bread and wine into His body and blood? If He can't do that, then He can't be God because "nothing is impossible with God." (Luke 1:37)

OK, so Jesus changed bread and wine into His body and blood. That was 2000 years ago, but what about now? Is the bread and wine of today just a symbol of Jesus' body and blood? Well now, that depends on who is doing the changing. What does that mean? Let's go back to the Scriptures. "Then taking the bread and giving thanks, He broke it and gave it to them, saying: 'This is My body to be given for you. Do this in remembrance of Me.' He did the same with the cup after eating, saying as He did so: 'This is the cup of the new covenant in My blood, which will be shed for you." (Luke 22:19-20) Jesus said, "Do this in remembrance of Me." By these words

He gave His disciples the power to change bread and wine into His body and blood. The Apostles became the first priests and bishops of Jesus' Church.

Peter became the leader of the Apostles, the first Pope. "And you," He said to them, 'who do you say that I am?' 'You are the Messiah,' Simon Peter answered, 'the Son of the living God!' Jesus replied, 'Blest are you, Simon son of Jonah! No mere man has revealed this to you, but My heavenly Father. I for My part declare to you, you are 'Rock,' and on this rock I will build My Church, and the jaws of death shall not prevail against it. I will entrust to you the keys of the kingdom of heaven. Whatever you declare bound on earth shall be bound in heaven; whatever you declare loosed on earth shall be loosed in heaven.'" (Matthew 16:15-19)

The power that Jesus bestowed on His Apostles who became the first bishops is passed down from bishop to bishop through the generations. The bishops have the power to ordain priests giving them the power to change bread and wine into the body and blood of Jesus Christ. This is called the *real presence* of Jesus in the Holy Eucharist which means that Jesus is really and truly present, body and blood, soul and divinity, under the appearance of bread and wine. Can all priests do this? No, only those who have been ordained by the bishops can.

Have there been changes since Jesus' time?

Have there been changes in the Church since the time of Jesus that have affected this power to change bread and wine into His body and blood? Some groups since the time of the Protestant Reformation have broken away from the Catholic Church. This started in the 16th century. Some have broken away with their bishops intact. Therefore, the line of ordination was not broken. They also have the real presence of Jesus in the Holy Eucharist. Others who have broken away from the Catholic Church did break the line of ordination of the bishops in which cases the power was not transferred and, as a result, there is no real presence of Jesus – the bread and wine, then, is just a symbol of Jesus' body and blood.

Is there any proof of the real presence of Jesus in the Holy Eucharist?

Actually there are many proofs of the *real presence* of Jesus in the Holy Eucharist. A few are explained here:

The Eucharistic Miracle at Lanciano – "In about the year 700, a Basilian monk in Lanciano, Italy had continuous doubts about the Real Presence of Christ in the Eucharist and begged God to remove the doubt from him. One day, as he was offering the Holy Sacrifice, following the words of consecration, the bread literally changed into Flesh and the wine into Blood. . .the changed substances were not consumed. The bread turned flesh and the Blood, which coagulated into five irregular globules, were placed in a precious ivory container, where they are preserved even to the present day at the Shrine in Lanciano.

Many years later, the Church, wanting to ascertain the true nature of the substances, requested modern scientists to examine them and give their verdict. In 1970 a team of medical experts was convened to begin the investigation. Professor Odoardo Linoli sent his message to the Director of the Shrine. . .*In the beginning was the Word. And the Word was made Flesh.* In 1971 the complete report stated that the analysis verified the following:

The Flesh is real flesh. The Blood is real blood.

The Flesh consists of the muscular tissue of the heart (myocardium).

The Flesh and Blood belong to the human species.

In the Blood were found proteins in the same normal proportions (percentage wise) as are found in the make-up of fresh normal blood.

In the Blood there were also found these minerals: chlorides, phosphorus, magnesium, potassium, sodium, and calcium.

The preservation of the Flesh and Blood, which were left in their natural state for twelve centuries (i.e. without any chemical preservatives) and exposed to the action of atmosphere and biological agents, remains an extraordinary phenomenon.

Science has given a certain and thorough response to the authenticity of the Eucharistic Miracle of Lanciano."[67]

This same miracle is reported in another source which takes it a step further: "The flesh remained intact, but the blood in the chalice soon divided into five pellets of unequal sizes and irregular nuggets. On a scale obtained by the Archbishop, it was discovered that one nugget weighed the same as all five together, two as much as any three, and the smallest as much as the largest. The Host and the five pellets were placed in a reliquary of artistic ivory. . .The ivory reliquary was replaced in 1713 by the one which now exhibits the two relics. This is a monstrance of finely sculptured silver and crystal."[68]

Does all this seem incredible to you? Does it seem impossible that the weight of one pellet was the same as all five together? It seems impossible to me also, but then I remember that we have a God Who specializes in the seemingly impossible and that nothing is impossible for God.

---

[67] "The Eucharistic Miracle at Lanciano," The Marian Helpers Bulletin, January – March, 1984, p. 3
[68] *Eucharistic Miracles*, Joan Carroll Cruz, pp. 3-4

Would you like another example?

In 1608 in Faverney, France on Pentecost Sunday, the Blessed Sacrament (Holy Eucharist) was exposed on the altar in a simple monstrance with two oil lamps burning before it. The doors were shut for the night. On Monday morning when the sacristan opened the doors, he found the church filled with smoke and flames on all sides of the altar. Quickly he got help and they put out the flames, and then they discovered that the monstrance was suspended in the air above the altar. News spread quickly and the villagers and priests from surrounding areas soon filled the church. Many people were in awe. Skeptics examined the miracle for themselves. The suspension lasted 33 hours. There were 54 depositions collected. . .the Archbishop decided that the miracle was authentic.[69]

Joan Carroll Cruz, who researched the phenomenon of these miracles, wrote the book *Eucharistic Miracles*. She explains 36 major Eucharistic miracles recorded and authenticated in Church history. These miracles include Hosts which have turned to flesh, Hosts which have survived under circumstances which should have caused the bread and wine to disintegrate, consecrated wine which turned into visible blood as well as many miracles which occurred after sacrilegious acts have been committed against the Holy Eucharist. Mrs. Cruz also tells of saints who have subsisted solely on the Eucharist without taking any other food for a number of years. There are other Eucharistic miracles as well. Hard to believe? Google Eucharistic Miracles on the Internet. Check out the many accounts and proofs for yourself.

How did the priest know this?

When Officer Jesse Romero was a rookie cop back in 1983, he went to a Catholic Conference where about 20,000 people were present. Near

---

69   Ibid, pp.162-163

What are Eucharistic Miracles?

the end of the conference, the priest processed in with the Blessed Sacrament (the real presence of the Body and Blood of Jesus Christ). He placed the Blessed Sacrament on an elevated table where it was visible to everyone. All the people knelt down in worship.

Suddenly the priest said, "Jesus wants to heal people who are addicted to violence. There are people here with guns, nun-chucks, weapons, brass knuckles, knives. In the name of Jesus, give up your violence. Come up and put your weapons here at the feet of Jesus." Officer Romero couldn't believe what he was hearing. Who was going to do that – put their weapons at the feet of Jesus? Incredulously, 200 plus people walked up and put their weapons before the Blessed Sacrament.

Then the priest said, "There are people here who are addicted to narcotics, coke, heroin, pcp, marijuana. You are living a double life. Bring up your narcotics and turn your life over to Christ." Officer Romero thought, "How can you say that?" Remarkably about 500 people brought up all kinds of narcotics and put them in a pile before the Blessed Sacrament. The priest continued, "There are people here addicted to pornography, to all kinds of sexual disorders. Surrender your life to Jesus Who has the power to set you free." Hundreds walked up and gave up pornographic paraphernalia. There was a mountain of magazines, guns, knives, narcotics.

Seeing that display, Officer Romero reasoned, "Wait a minute. If that's just bread in that Monstrance (the vessel that holds the Blessed Sacrament), there is no way that bread has the power to bring you to display your sins. Bread does not have that power. But if it *is Jesus* like the Catholic Church has said for 2000 years, then I understand why people right now are being set free of addictions because it is Jesus Who has the power to remove the shackles of sin." He sat there in 1983 and said, "This has to be Jesus. There is no way people would do this. They almost always deny their addictions. They will lie right in your face." He saw Christ.[70]

Why does God allow these miracles to happen?

God wants us to believe in the *real presence* of Jesus in the Holy Eucharist. He gave us Himself because He wanted to be here with us in physical form so that we can actually take Him into ourselves and become one with Him. God's love for us is so great that He wants to be with us constantly until the time when He takes us home to be with Him forever in heaven. Jesus said, "Teach them to carry out everything I have commanded you, and know that I am with you always, until the end of the world." (Matthew 28:20)

If your faith doesn't include the *real presence* of Jesus in the Holy Eucharist, does it make you think that maybe you are missing something? Check it out for yourself. Much can be found by Googling and searching *Eucharistic Miracles* on the Internet. You can also go to the Library. If you happen to know a Catholic priest, he can give you more information and explanation as to why this is really true. Checking it out and getting your questions answered certainly can't hurt, can it? Who knows – you may learn something really astounding that may change your life. If not, well you haven't lost anything by trying, have you?

---

70   *Life Changing Stories of the Eucharist,* Jesse Romero, Lighthouse Catholic Media CD, 2012

A Few Things To Consider

In almost nine cases out of ten, those who have once had Faith but now reject it, or claim that it does not make sense, are driven not by reasoning but by the way they are living.

Believe the incredible and you can do the impossible.

There is a world of difference between submitting to the Divine Will from sullenness and submitting it knowing that God is Supreme Wisdom and that some day we will know all that happened, happened for the best.

The modern atheist does not disbelieve because of his intellect, but because of his will; it is not knowledge that makes him an atheist. . .The denial of God springs from a man's desire not to have a God – from his wish that there were no Justice behind the universe so that his injustices would fear not retribution; from his desire that there be no Law, so that he may not be judged by it; from his wish that there were no Absolute Goodness, that he might go on sinning with impunity. That is why the modern atheist is always angered when he hears anything said about God and religion – he would be incapable of such a resentment if God were only a myth.

The Wisdom Of Fulton Sheen, Introduction by Matthew Kelly, Blue Sparrow Publications, North Palm Beach, FL, pp. 29, 45, 71, 119

VI

Where Are We?
Are We Done?

Chapter 1

Do We Know God Better Now?

Is God less of a mystery now?

God, Who is Father, Jesus the Son, and Holy Spirit is One. There is no other. If there were other gods, then none would be god because God of necessity has to be above all else otherwise He could not be God. God knows all things. God is all-powerful. Nothing is impossible for God. God is all good and all that He has created is good. God is in control of *all* things at *all* times. Nothing happens without His knowledge or without His permission. God is Love.

God created angels and humankind and gave us free will. Some of the angels turned against God, and with full knowledge of the consequences of their actions, because of their pride, refused to serve Him. They lost their place in heaven and are banned for all eternity.

Humankind, Adam and Eve, disobeyed God, did not have full realization of the consequences of their sin, and were banned from the beautiful Garden of Eden that God had created for them. God in His infinite love and mercy promised to send a Redeemer. Evil, which is the absence of good, entered the world. Why does God allow evil? Dr. Eban Alexander explained for us, "Evil was necessary because without it free will was impossible, and without free will could be no growth – no chance for us to become what God longed for us to be. . .love was overwhelmingly dominant, and it would ultimately be triumphant. "[71] Also, Mary C. Neal, M.D. tells us "Without observing cruelty, we would not be moved to compassion. Without personal trials, we would not develop patience or faithfulness. . .our earthly concerns matter little when compared to life eternal that allows us to know joy in the midst of sorrow and worry."[72] God allows evil to take place, but He always turns it into something good. We don't always see this or understand it, but God knows what He has in mind. God is love and He cares for all that He has created. He cares for **all His children**. God is Love.

How do we know that God loves us?

God not only tells us Himself, He proves His love for us. How does He tell us of His love and care for us? Read the Bible. From beginning to end, the Bible is one long, beautiful love letter from God to His people, not just to the Israelites, but to each one, to you and to me. As a loving Parent, God tells us of His love; He instructs us as to how we should live, following His command-ments. Those who follow His commandments and are obedient live truly happy lives. You are not sure about this? Read the lives of the saints. No matter what hardships they may have had to face, they did it with complete trust in God and were filled with joy. Hard to understand? Not really.

---

71 *Proof of Heaven A Neurosurgeon's Journey into the Afterlife*, Eban Alexander, M.D., pp.47-48

72 *To Heaven And Back*, Mary C, Neal, MD, Waterback Press, Division of Random House, New York, p. 100

Why? Because they were filled with peace and knew that they would eventually go to a better place.

How Does God show us that He loves us?

God created us. Did He need us? No. Why did He create us? God is love and He wanted to share His love beyond Himself, beyond Father, Son, and Holy Spirit. He created angels and the human race and possibly other beings in the vast universe of which we know nothing about.

God came Himself, in the person of Jesus Christ to Earth for the purpose of revealing Himself to us and to save us from our sins. How did He do that? By His life, Jesus taught us about God's love for us. He taught us to be kind and compassionate, merciful, and forgiving. He gave us many proofs that He is indeed the Son of God through His healings and miracles. Most importantly, He taught us about God's mercy. Jesus suffered and died offering His own body and blood as a payment for our sins. He didn't have to do that, but His love for us is so great that He willingly laid down His own life that we might have eternal life and happiness in heaven. What further proof could there possibly be of His unconditional love?

Is there more? Yes. Jesus left His very self in the sacrament of the Holy Eucharist, His own Body and Blood for us. He said to His disciples, "Teach them to carry out everything I have commanded you. *And know that I am with you always, <u>until the end of the world</u>.*" (Matthew 28:20) He founded The Church to help and guide us.

More still? Jesus sent us His Holy Spirit, the Spirit of Truth, to guide the Church and to be our Advocate, to help us in all our needs, and to lead us in the love of God and of our neighbor. Could there be any doubt that God loves us?

Does God love *everyone*?

Are there any exclusions? God loves:

Those who obey His commandments, are faithful to Him, and put complete trust in Him. To these He grants their heart's desires.

Those who sincerely search for Him. He assists them on their journey and leads them to the truth, to Himself.

Those who suffer, the sick, the broken hearted, those with heavy burdens, those who struggle. He gives them the strength and endurance they need. He brings them the healing they need, spiritual, emotional, physical.

Those who grieve Him by their sinful lives, the thieves, the murderers, the fornicators, the abortionists, the adulterers, the terrorists, etc., even the corrupt governmental officials. He has given us free will and allows them to reap the consequences of their sins. He pursues them lovingly and gives them every grace to overcome their slavery to sin and to reconcile themselves to Him. The choice is theirs.

Those who don't know Him. He gives all people the chance to know Him by following the dictates of their heart and to live accordingly.

The agnostics who are not sure that there is a God, the atheists who deny that there is a God, and those who are not sure what or who to believe. He pursues them and gives them every opportunity to come to know Him. Again, the choice is theirs.

God loves everyone – no one, **no one is excluded.** Each one of His children is precious to Him. God is very much grieved by the loss of any one of His children.

How do we know just how merciful God is?

How many times have we disobeyed God's commandments? Even the most holy of people have sinned. We are all sinners. Some of the greatest saints were at one time among the worst of sinners – remember St. Augustine? Just how many times will God forgive us? Remember the abortionists who snuffed out thousands of innocent babies' lives, then repented of their horrible sins? Is God willing to forgive all this? Yes, He is. He suffered and died for that purpose. Jesus tells us, "I tell you, there will likewise be more joy in heaven over one repentant sinner than over ninety-nine righteous people who have no need to repent." (Luke 15:7)

Will God forgive you no matter who you are?

We find the answer in the Bible – "My little ones, I am writing this to keep you from sin. But if anyone should sin, we have, in the presence of the Father, Jesus Christ, an intercessor Who is just. He is an offering for our sins, and not for our sins only, but for those of the whole world." (1John 2:1-2) God is good and merciful to all. He loves each and every one of us and desires our salvation so much so that He Himself paid the price for our sins in the person of Jesus Christ. And what a price! Believe it. It is true!

What does God want from us?

Obedience – we are to obey His commandments. Why else would He give them to us? They are meant for our own good so that we may have a better more fulfilling and much happier life. God wants us to love Him and to love each other. Jesus said, "As the Father has loved

Me, so I have loved you. Live on in My love. You will live in My love if you keep My commandments, even as I have kept My Father's commandments, and live in His love. All this I tell you that My joy may be yours and your joy may be complete. This is My commandment: love one another as I have loved you. There is no greater love than to lay down one's life for one's friends." (John 15:9-13)

Do you remember – we said that following God's commandments is much easier than not? Life is much easier – it keeps you out of trouble, you won't carry the burden of guilt, you will be healthier, you will be happier, and most of all you will inherit eternal life. This life is only for a short duration, usually less than 100 years. Eternity goes on forever. Don't you want to spend eternity with God in beauty and happiness? I sure do. Now that is what I call a **win-win** situation. Don't you agree?

> **"Yes, God so loved the world that He gave His only Son that**
> **whoever believes in Him may not die**
> **But may have eternal life.**
> **God did not send His Son into the world**
> **To condemn the world,**
> **But that the world might be**
> **Saved through Him."**
> *(John 3:16-17)*

Chapter 2

Where Do We Go From Here?

What is needed at this time?

Look around you. What is happening in your immediate circle, your family, your friends, your neighbors, your community? Who is it that needs your help? What can you do to help? If your answer is "nothing" or "not much," think again. If a problem appears to be beyond the scope of what you can do, you can always pray, ask the Holy Spirit for guidance, and put your complete trust in God. Jesus assures us that, "if you had faith the size of a mustard seed... Nothing would be impossible for you." (Matthew 17:20) Nothing would be impossible for you? That is quite a claim. Has it happened? Many times. There are a number of true stories throughout this book where the "impossible" happened. Check out for yourself a number of incredible true stories in the library, at the bookstore, or on the Internet. You will find amazing true accounts of unbelievable occurrences for which there is no possible explanation.

God is always there for you. All you need do is to call upon Him. His help comes not too soon nor too late, but just at the right time. As a loving Father, He knows and always does what is best at the time.

Is Jesus compassionate and there for us in our distress? Jesus lovingly assures us, "Come to Me, all you who are weary and find life burdensome, and I will refresh you. Take My yoke upon your shoulders and learn from Me, for I am gentle and humble of heart. Your souls will find rest, for My yoke is easy and My burden light." (Matthew 11:28-30) Who else can promise this?

Who else is there for you in your time of need? People will come and go in your life, but God is steadfast. He is *always* there and will never leave you. If there are times when He seems to be far away, ask yourself — who was it that moved? You?

What is the meaning of my life?

Why did God create *ME?* Why am I here? Life should be joyful and happy. Does that sound unrealistic to you? Not so. You can have a happy life. If there is unhappiness in your life, chances are that someone is not obeying God's commandments. If it is you, change your ways. If it is someone close to you, pray for that person. True happiness in this life can only come by focusing your life on God. All material things come to an end – money, property, goods, power. None of these will go with you when you die. Everything, *everything* is left behind. "Have no love for the world, the Father's love has no place in him, for nothing that the world affords comes from the Father. . .And the world with all its seductions is passing away but the man who does God's will endures forever." (1 John 2:15-17) "A phantom only, man goes his ways; like vapor only are his restless pursuits; he heaps up stores, and knows not who will use them." (Psalm 39:7)

Let your focus then, be on life eternal. How? Simple – "The way we can be sure of our knowledge of Him is to keep His commandments. The man who claims, 'I have known Him,' without keeping His commandments, is a liar; in such a one there is no truth." (1 John

2:3-4) "Beloved, if our consciences have nothing to charge us with, we can be sure that God is with us and that we will receive at His hands *whatever we ask*. Why? Because we are keeping His commandments and doing what is pleasing in His sight. His commandment is this: we are to believe in the name of His Son, Jesus Christ, and are to love one another as He commanded us." (1 John 3:21-23)

Therefore, the meaning of my life is to love God by keeping His commandments, and to love my neighbor, and to love all of God's creation because it is all very good. When this life on earth is done, how wonderful it will be to spend eternity with God and all those loving people in glorious beauty and happiness that can never fade nor be taken away.

What else is necessary?

What is happening in our country, in the world? Can't you see what is going on – all the injustices, all the corruption on all levels of government? Jesus said to the crowds, "You hypocrites!. . .why do you not judge for yourselves what is just?" (Luke 12:56-57) What is Jesus telling us? With all the corruption and injustices taking place all around us, we need to read the signs of the times and take action to counteract the wrongs perpetrated against society.

How can I do that? I am not a person in power, nor am I a person of influence. I am not a politician. I'm one of the "little people" to whom no one will listen. If enough "little people" get together to make their voices heard, something has to be done. Our American people are fed up with left-wing politicians eroding bit by bit the government set in place by our founding fathers. The Constitution is being twisted and interpreted in ways that were never intended. Our freedoms are being stolen from us, and we need to stand up for our beliefs, for our Country, and for our God.

We have already lost too much. We can no longer pray in public. Prayer has been taken out of public schools. Roe v. Wade has been overturned returning the abortion issue back to the states where it belongs. However, the battle still rages on – a number of people still want to murder the unborn baby. Parental rights are being subverted, allowing school personnel to groom children in transgender programs without the knowledge of the parent. Biological men who transgender into women are allowed to compete in women's sports giving them an unfair advantage against women athletes. Gangs and crime has escalated to an all-time high because of defunding the Police. We, the taxpayers, are being forced to pay for people who don't want to work, for "rights" of illegal aliens who come here to take advantage of programs set in place to help our poor. There are people who come here carrying flags from other countries, who don't want to assimilate into our culture, who expect us to learn their language. Our borders at present are wide open. People come from all over the world expecting us to hand them food, housing, schooling, medical care, etc. – all at the expense of the American taxpayer. We have our own problems that need to be addressed – homelessness, flood disasters, tornado damage, drugs pouring over our border poisoning and killing our young people. What about our military that has been decimated and our veterans that are in need of care? Did I <u>miss</u> anything? Probably. Oh yes, what about the amount of useless government spending that will plague our children for many years to come? Where is the justice in all these things.

What else do we need to consider?

We need to respect the dignity of each human person made in the image and likeness of God. We need to recognize the intrinsic worth of each human person – that means the unborn child as well. We need to get out from under the holocaust of abortion that is dragging our country down. Roe v. Wade has been overturned and the power returned to the states where it rightfully belongs. However, the battle still rages on with some states continuing their gruesome practice of promoting abortion. God Himself is the Master of life and death, no one else. Having the audacity to assume God's role will have dire consequences. What can a person say when facing the Eternal Creator at the end of his/her life? Don't be so foolish as to put yourself in that position. Hellfire is not fun. Don't fool yourself into thinking that hell does not exist. We will all be held accountable for our transgressions. Some people may choose not to believe all this. Are you one of them? That is your choice according to the free will given to us by God. What happens if you are wrong? Think about **that!** Where will *you* end up?

At present our country the United States of America seems to be falling apart. We need to get down on our knees and beg God for His help. We want the USA to remain as **ONE NATION UNDER GOD** with liberty and justice for all.

**I pledge allegiance to the Flag of the
United States of America
And to the Republic for which it stands,
ONE NATION UNDER GOD,
Indivisible, with liberty and justice for all.**

VII

Conclusion – What's in it for You and for Me?

CONCLUSION

What Can We Expect?

What can we expect from God?

God is true to His promises; He can neither deceive nor be deceived. On our journey through this book, we have experienced God's goodness and love in all that He does for us. He helps us in ways of which we are mostly unaware. How often do we thank Him for all that He does? We have discovered how to trust Him more by better understanding that He knows and *always* does what is best for us as any loving Father would do. Life has its ups and downs, good times, and times that are frustrating, not so good. Some days are so wonderful and so enjoyable, yet they don't last, they fade; but neither do the difficult days last. Everything comes to an end sooner or later. Only one thing in life remains constant, that lasts – **the love of God.**

But there is more. God is merciful. Look back at all the circumstances in your life and all the situations in which sin has played a part. Perhaps you were chained to a particular sin in your life such as lying, promiscuity, stealing, etc. Did God in His wrath strike you dead? Obviously not or you would not be here reading this book.

Sin is abhorrent to God. Did you deserve His anger? You probably did. So why are you still here? Because God loves you **unconditionally and desires your salvation**. For that reason He is very patient with you and with me, and with all His children. We have learned that He gives each person the time and graces needed to come to our senses and turn our life around so that we may inherit eternal life. The choice is ours to accept or to reject God's love and grace. If He was willing to come down from heaven Himself in the person of Jesus Christ, will He not also give us everything we need and also what we desire to have, provided it will not be to the detriment of our eternal soul? God's mercy is His greatest attribute. Avail yourself of it. You don't want to lose out on the greatest adventure of your existence that is yet to come, do you?

What is this great adventure all about?

St. Paul says, "Eye has not seen, ear has not heard, nor has it so much as dawned on man what God has prepared for those who love Him." (1 Corinthians 2:9)

Wow! We can't even begin to imagine what God has in store for us, all the beauty, all the wonder. Finding out all the secrets of the Universe as well as all about our own planet Earth, what an incredible adventure that will be. All the intellectual, analytical scientific minds of the human race will be ecstatic to finally learn all that God has created and how it all works. Fantastic! If you look up at the night sky and see all the stars and how many solar systems God has created, not to mention what we can't see, do you ever wonder what else is out there? I don't think that it is all there just to look nice. Are there other beings that God created? Will we meet them? What an enlightenment! I mean to find out. I know one thing – I do not want to miss out on any of it. What about you?

And what about all our earthlings?

Won't it be exciting to meet in person all the great and wonderful people that we could only read about in history books or biographical accounts? I look forward to meeting such people as George Washington. I want to know his story and how he helped to forge our great country, the United States of America and how he dedicated it to God. I want to meet St. Mother Teresa of Calcutta, whom I had actually seen in person and heard her speak, such an inspiration to so many people. What was most appealing about her was that she accepted *everyone* regardless of his/her beliefs, much as God does. Is this unconditional love or what? Wouldn't you like to meet her? I sure would. The brilliant mind of St. Thomas Aquinas, who was able to understand and remember everything he ever read, always intrigued me. The courage of Edith Stein to her Jewish people for whom she offered and gave up her very life, excites me. She is now a saint of the Catholic Church. What about Abraham, Isaac, Jacob, Moses, David and all the great patriarchs, Isaiah, Jeremiah, and all the other great prophets? How fascinating to know first-hand their complete stories. I also want to know the great sinners like St. Augustine, remember him? And even Ted Bundy who murdered all those women but found mercy and forgiveness from the Lord, and was able to have salvation.

All that we read and know is just a sliver of what actually happened. How exhilarating to meet everyone who ever lived and are now in the kingdom of heaven, to get to know their stories of how they came to know to love God and to accept His graces in order to have eternal life. How long will it take to get to know all these wonderful people which, by the way, incudes you, your family members, your friends and neighbors, and everyone you have ever crossed paths with, or only met on the Internet while you were on earth – all these people who have accepted God's grace? Who cares how long it takes? We have forever – eternity without end – to get to know each other, and that's a l-o-n-g, l-o-n-g, l-o-n-g "time."!!!

How is all this possible?

It is possible because of God's great love and mercy towards us. We have a loving Father. We should be forever grateful to Jesus Who came to earth and paid the price for *our* sins. Without the tremendous sacrifice of His own life, where would we be? We need to thank Jesus every day for that. We have the Holy Spirit Who guides us, gives us the courage and power to accomplish wonderful things. We need to praise and thank God every day for His goodness to us. We need to begin **right now** if we haven't already done so. Don't you agree?

And what will be the most glorious event ever?

That one should be easy. What is your guess? I think that meeting God Himself, face to face, will be the most wondrous of all experiences. Why? Because then I can really see the wonderful Father that I have, the Father Who designed me, took care of me, protected me, and helped me to grow in His love. I will see Jesus, the Son of God, Who came to earth to save *me* in spite of all my sins, as undeserving as I am. Why? Just because He loves me, that's all. I don't deserve it; I didn't earn it. He just loves *me* and *you*, too. That's it? Yes, that's it! I will tell Him how eternally grateful I am for that, and I will praise Him forever. I will see the Holy Spirit Who inspired me, enlightened me, steered me on the right path, and helped me to get to the glorious gate of heaven. I will also see our Blessed Mother Mary and all the saints who helped me in so many ways through their intercession. And of course, I will see my family and friends and be united with them forever. There is nothing more that anyone could desire. How do you feel about all this? Give praise, honor, and glory to God forever and ever!

WHAT CAN WE EXPECT?

Do you recognize any of these scenarios in your life?

Perhaps reading this book will start you thinking about *your* life and where you are headed in your journey toward eternity.

Could it be that you are enslaved in an illicit relationship and are now encouraged to break those chains?

Are you stuck in prison because of bad choices you made and are now experiencing hope for forgiveness?

Suffering with an illness, maybe you came to realize how it is bringing you closer to God.

By giving this book to your son or daughter who may not be living according to God's laws, you are hoping it will make a difference.

Perhaps you are not a Christian but are now curious about the teachings of Jesus and desire to know more about God's great love.

Is it possible that you think this is all hogwash and don't believe any of it? Try rereading it again sometime and really think about what it means *for your own sake.* It could make an eternal difference.

So, if you have a spouse, son or daughter, relative or friend for whom you are concerned regarding the state of his/her immortal soul and his/her eternal salvation, pray for that person. Give him/her a copy of this book to read as it has the power to change hearts. If nothing else, it will offer encouragement and hope to the most depressed and abject person learning that God, the Creator of the Universe loves him/her regardless of all the sins he/she may have committed.

Anyone can have salvation if he/she but turns to God with a sincere heart. God's love and mercy is far greater than any sin regardless of how many there are. God's love is unconditional. God desires the salvation of all His children. **No one, no one is excluded.**

Did you figure it out?

Do you know why I have written this book? Is it crystal clear to you now? Just in case you are not sure, I am going to spell it out for you. I wrote this for *you* to contemplate the great worth and condition of your own soul. The reason is that I desire the salvation of *your soul.*

You may be wondering why I desire the salvation of your soul because chances are that I don't even know you and will never meet you or even know your name. If that's what you think, then let me tell you that you are wrong. How is that? I plan to meet you in person. How? When? Where? Why? I plan to meet you in eternity, in heaven, because I want to get to know you. I want to hear your story. Perhaps you will say to me, "I read your book, and it started me thinking that I would be foolish not to check out God and His love for *me*. So, I did and now here I am. After reading your book and contemplating the most important essence of my being, I decided that I want to enjoy **forever** all the wonders that God has in store for **me**. Then I passed your book on to my family members and friends, and they are here, too. Would you like to meet them, also?" Of course, I would love to meet your family and friends. Is my message *that important*? You better believe it. Your eternal destiny or that of someone you love may depend on it.

Yes, my reason is that I want as many people as possible to have salvation because I want to meet them all. Is that kind of selfish of me? Perhaps. But it will be a very happy selfishness. It is like the Pacific Ocean. Every drop is important. If even one drop is missing, then the ocean is incomplete. Don't let that drop be you. Remember, there are many paths to God. Some paths are easier than others. Make sure that you find the right path for you.

Let's make an appointment right now to meet in eternity. I look forward to meeting **you** there. Don't disappoint me. I plan to be there. Make sure that you are there, too. Until we meet, may God bless you and keep you in His loving care, God Who is Father, Jesus the Son, and the Holy Spirit.

> **"The Lord bless you and keep you!**
> **The Lord let His face shine upon you**
> **And be gracious to you!**
> **The Lord look upon you kindly**
> **And give you peace!"**

(Numbers 6:24-26)

By the way while reading this book, did you happen to notice that God pursues people because He loves each one of us? He finds ways to alert a person to pay attention to His clues because He wants every one of His children to have salvation and happiness with Him forever in heaven.

Did you also notice that many times God does this through other people? There are many good people in this world who are willing to help other people in times of natural disasters, wars, food shortages, needs for clean water, in times of illnesses, and other needs. Our Military Forces, Police, Firefighters, First Responders, Medical Personnel, etc. are always ready to help. But there are also many other ordinary people, not professionals, who see a need and jump right in to help in any need.

Why is that? That is the Holy Spirit inspiring a person who sees a need and to respond. And these people do respond. They are not looking for any kind of reward, they just do it because it is the right thing to do. That's God's goodness working through them. God works through people.

Next time you happen to see someone helping another person in need, thank God for the kindness of that helper. Say a special prayer for him/her. Look around. These people are everywhere. Some day you may need help. Will there be a person there for you? You bet there will be. God is so good; He will provide the help you need probably *through another person*.

Appendix A

The Ten Commandments

What do they mean? (Exodus 20:1-17)

1. *I, the Lord, am your God, who brought you out of the land of Egypt, that place of slavery. You shall not have other gods besides Me.*

"You shall worship the Lord your God and Him only shall you serve." (Matthew 4:10) It is forbidden to make any graven image nor any likeness of anything that flies in the sky such as birds, nor anything on the earth including all kinds of animals, snakes, or crawling things, nor anything in the water. You shall not bow down to worship them. Nor shall you worship any human person. You shall worship God alone. There is no other. The first commandment requires us to nourish and protect our faith and to reject everything that is opposed to it.[73]

---

73   *Catechism of the Catholic Church*, Part Three, p. 506, 2088

We are to put our hope and trust in God. By **despair** one ceases to hope for his/her personal salvation believing his/her sins will not be forgiven – not trusting in God. **Presumption** is relying on one's own ability for salvation without God's help or presuming on God's mercy without conversion of heart – that is turning away from one's sins.[74] One can also sin against God's love by neglecting or refusing to accept God's goodness and care, by being ungrateful and not returning love to God – hatred of God.[75]

The first commandment also forbids superstitious beliefs, spells, charms, mediums (people who claim to converse with or contact the dead), witchcraft, sorcery, spiritists, and fortunetellers. These are wrong and sinful because believing in them invests in them a power that they do not and cannot have, a power that belongs to God alone.

2. *You shall not take the name of the Lord your God in vain. "For the Lord will not leave unpunished him who takes His name in vain." (Exodus 20:7)*

What does taking God's name in vain mean? That would be using God's name without reverence such as cursing or using it in a light, careless manner as in an exclamation. God's name is holy. The name of Jesus Christ, the Son of God, is holy. All honor and respect must be given to this holy name. Yet, how many times do you hear it uttered in anger, or annoyance, or surprise?

Sometimes it is necessary to use God's name such as to swear in court testifying to the truth of what one is about to state. Falsely swearing by God's name, lying under oath is called **perjury**, is offensive to God, and also carries penalties such as a jail sentence.

---

74 Ibid, Part Three, p. 507, 2091-2092
75 Ibid, Part Three, p. 508, 2094

Persons in authority to govern and enforce our laws according to our Constitution take an oath. This is the proper use of God's holy name to promise to uphold lawful authority.

Blasphemy is the use of any words or actions deliberately intended to insult God.

3. Remember to keep holy the Sabbath day. *(Exodus 20:8)*

God blessed the seventh day and made it holy because He rested from all the work He had done in creation.

By this commandment we are to take one day a week, Saturday or Sunday, depending on your faith, to worship God. Also, it is a day of rest from our labor. We are permitted to take part in recreational and non-laborious activities. We can, however, do servile or bodily work when our need or the need of another requires it, such as the duties of hospital or nursing home employees or if you work at a place where your employer requires you to be there.

4. Honor your father and your mother. *(Exodus 20:12)*

Our parents are the first people we perceive as loving us. The kind of love they show to us is the kind of love we will reflect throughout the rest of our life in most cases. We should treat our parents with respect. As children we need to obey them. As adults and as our parents age, we should see to their care providing for their material and spiritual needs – taking care of them in sickness, helping them in their needs, spending time with them. If they were abusive or controlling, we need to forgive them as best as we can. Forgiving them will also lighten our burden of any ill will we carry toward them. And we need to pray for them.

5. *You shall not kill. (Exodus 20:13)*

The taking of the life of an innocent person made in the image and likeness of God is abhorrent to God. This is murder. God is the Master of life and death. Murder also includes **abortion** which is the deliberate termination by force of the life of an unborn child.

Euthanasia or mercy killing is a deliberate termination of the life of a sick, dying, or handicapped person. It is not OK to end the life of a person who is suffering with excruciating pain either by direct action or deliberate omission of an action with the intention of causing the death of the person. However, it is permissible to disconnect **extraordinary** means of preserving life.

Killing can only be justified if someone physically attacks you; you have the right to defend yourself. "Human life can lawfully be taken in self-defense, in a just war, or by the lawful execution of a criminal fairly tried and found guilty of a crime punishable by death when the preservation of law and order and the good of the community requires such execution.[76]

The fifth commandment also prohibits disrespect for the dignity of persons. This includes scandal which is an attitude or behavior which leads another to sin, the decline of morals, social conditions that make obedience to the commandments difficult or impossible, provoking someone to anger, the manipulation of public opinion to turn others away from moral values.

We are to take reasonable care of our body by avoiding every kind of excess – the **abuse** of food, alcohol, tobacco, drugs, and even medicines, endangering one's self or another by speeding on the road.

Kidnapping and hostage taking, anger with a desire for revenge as well as deliberate hatred against a person, racial discrimination –

---

[76] *Catechism of Christian Doctrine*, Rev. Thomas L. Kinkead, p. 287

these are grave offences against the fifth commandment that can lead to bodily harm or even death.

6. *You shall not commit adultery. (Exodus 20:14)*
9. *You shall not covet your neighbor's wife. (Exodus 20:17)*

These two commandments, the sixth and the ninth, are closely related. "The only lawful and chaste use of sex is its lawful use in marriage. Lust is the vice of indulging unlawful sexual pleasures."[77]

"Adultery refers to marital infidelity. When two partners, of whom at least one is married to another party have sexual relations, they commit adultery."[78] This is a very grave sin, an injustice done to the other spouse. It causes much pain and suffering to the spouse and damage to the family unit. The children seem to suffer most of all.

Some offences against these two commandments include:

> Fornication – is carnal union between an unmarried man and an unmarried woman and is gravely contrary to their dignity and to the sacrament of Matrimony.
>
> Pornography – is displaying real or simulated sexual acts. It does grave injury to the dignity of its participants. It is highly addictive and has led some who have engaged in child pornography into incarceration.
>
> Prostitution – does injury to the dignity of the persons involved reducing them to instruments of sexual pleasure and opening them up to diseases.

---

[77]   *A Tour of the Summa,* Msgr. Paul J Glenn, p. 280
[78]   "Adultery," *Catechism of the Catholic Church, p. 572*

Incest – is intimate relations between relatives and corrupts family relationships.

Sexual abuse of children – does physical, moral, and psychological harm to the child scarring him/her for life.

Free union – is living together without marriage commitment and exhibits a lack of trust in each other.

Homosexual activity – relations between persons of the same sex. Sacred Scripture condemns this as acts of grave depravity.

Masterbation – is the deliberate stimulation of the genital organs for the purpose of deriving sexual pleasure.

Sex outside of marriage has psychological, emotional, relational, and physical consequences including sexually transmitted diseases (STD).

7. *You shall not steal. (Exodus 20:15)*

10. *You shall not covet your neighbor's goods. (Exodus 20:17)*

The seventh and tenth commandments are also closely related.

". . .respect for human dignity requires. . .temperance, so as to moderate attachment to this world's goods; justice, to preserve our neighbor's rights and render him what is his due."[79]

The seventh commandment forbids theft – usurping another's property against the reasonable will of the owner.

---

[79] *Catechism of the Catholic Church*, Part Three, p. 578, 2407

Promises must be kept and contracts strictly observed. Reparation for injustice committed requires return of the stolen goods to their owner.

Games of chance or wagers in themselves are not contrary to justice but become morally unacceptable when they deprive someone of what is necessary to provide for his needs.

Gambling risks, unfair wagers, and cheating at games constitute a grave matter. Acts or enterprises that lead to the enslavement of human beings, their being bought or sold is a sin against the dignity of persons.

Animals are God's creatures and must be treated with kindness.[80]

Refusing or withholding a just wage is a grave injustice.

The tenth commandment forbids greed and the desire to amass earthly goods without limit.

Envy refers to sadness at the sight of another's goods and the desire to acquire them for oneself even unjustly.

Wishing harm to a neighbor is sinful.

Also forbidden is avarice arising from a passion for riches and their power.[81]

8. *You shall not bear false witness against your neighbor. (Exodus 20:16)*

Lying is speaking a falsehood with the intention of deceiving someone who has the right to know the truth. Offences against the truth requires reparation.

---

80   Ibid, Part Three, p. 580, 2413-2415
81   Ibid, Part Three, p. 606, 607, 2536-2539

Professional secrets and confidences must be kept. Society has a right to information based on the truth. Civil authorities have particular responsibilities because of the common good.

Journalists have the obligation to disseminate truth while not offending against charity using respect in their reporting.

False witness and **perjury** under oath is especially grave compromising justice and the fairness of judicial decisions.

Respect for one's reputation forbids attitudes or words likely to cause unjust injury. This includes **detraction** – disclosing the faults and failings of another; **calumny** – remarks contrary to the truth causing harm to the reputation of another; **rash judgment** – assuming as true without knowledge the moral fault of another.[82]

Note: For a more indepth explanation of each of the commandments, refer to the *Catechism of the Catholic Church*, Liguori Publications, One Liguori Drive, Liguori, MO 63057-9999, ISBN 0-89243-566-6, Part Three, Section Two: The Ten Commandments, pages 505-611

---

82   Ibid, Part Three, p. 594-597

Appendix B

Mary Mother Of God

Who is Mary?

Simply put – Mary is the Daughter of God the Father.
Mary is the Mother of Jesus Christ, the Son of God.
Mary is the Spouse of the Holy Spirit.

Mary the Daughter of God the Father, the First Person of the Holy Trinity

When Adam and Eve sinned against God by disobeying His command, they were banished from the beautiful Garden of Eden and lost God's grace not only for themselves but for all of their descendants as well. However, God did not abandon humankind. He promised to send a Redeemer Who would restore the human race to His grace.

God planned to come Himself as a human to pay the price for our sins in order to restore our lost grace. Therefore, He needed a human person to be His mother and to help Him grow from a baby into manhood. Not just any woman would do. Since God is sinless, He needed a mother who would be sinless as no sin could ever touch God.

God created a sinless virgin, the Virgin Mary who from her conception in her mother's womb was filled with Sanctifying Grace and was free from the supernatural effects of original sin that came down from Adam and Eve. This is called the Immaculate Conception.[83] Because of this *special privilege,* Mary remained pure and unable to ever sin.

Mary the Spouse of the Holy Spirit, the Third Person of the Holy Trinity

"Now in the sixth month the angel Gabriel was sent from God to a town of Galilee called Nazareth to a virgin betrothed to a man named Joseph, of the house of David, and the virgin's name was Mary. And when the angel had come to her, he said, 'Hail, full of grace, the Lord is with thee. Blessed art thou among women. She was troubled at his word and kept pondering what manner of greeting this might be. . .the angel said to her, 'Do not be afraid, Mary, for thou hast found grace with God. Behold, thou shalt conceive in thy womb and shalt bring forth a son, and thou shalt call His name Jesus. He shall be great, and shall be called the Son of the Most High, and the Lord God will give Him the throne of David His father and He shall be king over the house of Jacob forever, and of His kingdom there shall be no end.' But Mary said to the angel, 'How shall this happen since I do not know man?' And the angel answered and said to her, 'The Holy Spirit shall come upon thee and the power of the Most High shall overshadow thee, and therefore the Holy One to be born shall be called the Son of God. . .for nothing shall be impossible with God.' But Mary said, 'Behold the handmaid of the Lord; be it done to me according to thy

---

83   O'Laverty, Fr. H., B.A., *The Mother of God and Her Glorious Feasts,* Tan Books and Publishers, Inc., Rockford, IL, p. 4

word.' And the angel departed from her." (Luke 1:26-38) By Mary's consent did the Son of God come incarnate into the world.

Mary the mother of Jesus Christ, the Son of God, the Second Person of the Holy Trinity

Jesus Christ the Son of God came to earth in human form as a baby, born of a human mother, Mary. He is fully God and fully human. He paid the price for our sins through His suffering, crucifixion, death, and resurrection from the dead thus restoring us to grace and reconciliation with God so that we may inherit eternal life with Him in heaven. His mother Mary was an integral part of His suffering. She knew everything He was going through and suffered along with Him more so than any mother suffers with her hurting child.

When Jesus was dying on the cross, He gave His mother Mary to us to be our mother when He said, "Woman behold thy son" to John, His disciple. (John 19:26) It was then that Mary understood that she was to be the spiritual mother of all God's children.

How does all this affect you and me?

The Blessed Virgin Mary is a most loving mother who cares for and helps all her children. All one needs to do is to ask her. She guides, helps us in our needs, and always leads us to her Divine Son Jesus. Throughout history she has appeared to many individuals giving instructions and telling them to pray for the world and for the salvation of souls. People need to stop sinning against God's commandments.

The Blessed Virgin Mary has given warnings as to what would take place if her words were not heeded.

In 1917, Mary appeared to three shepherd children in Fatima, Portugal. Mary warned of the consequences of unrepented sin – Hell in the afterlife, and in this life the punishment of nations. (See Section V, Chapter 2, page 194) She showed Hell to the children and spoke about a new world war (World War II) and that communism would spread if people did not amend their ways and turn to God. Jesus wants devotion to the Immaculate Heart of Mary through the recitation of the Rosary as well as other devotions. To prove the authenticity of Mary's words, the Miracle of the Sun took place and was witnessed by 70,000 people. The Blessed Mother clearly stated that wars, as well as other disasters such as tornadoes, floods, earthquakes, and other natural disasters are a punishment for the sins of nations. God's severe chastisements are meant to correct and bring about the conversion of sinners so that they may *choose* salvation.

Take a look around you. What do you see? – Broken families, unfaithful spouses, disrespectful disobedient children, lying, drug and substance abuse, smash and grab theft, homelessness, rape, frequent shootings in schools and religious houses of worship, assaults and murders, slaughter of the innocents through abortion, all kinds of white-collar crimes such as fraud and money manipulation, transgender mutilation of children. Did I miss anything? Probably. Is it any wonder that God is angry?

Is there hope?

In spite of all this, God still loves all His children and wants to give us a remedy through devotion to the Immaculate Heart of Mary that will lessen the severity. Yes, there will be wars and natural disasters to chastise the world to bring about conversion. However, the Blessed Virgin Mary assures us – "In the end my Immaculate Heart will triumph and there will be peace."

Appendix C

The Abortion Issue

How could this happen?

In our United States of America, on January 22, 1973, the Supreme Court ruled and struck down all laws enacted in every state that protected the lives of unborn children. It legalized abortion-on-demand through all nine months of pregnancy in all 50 states. In essence, the Court declared a baby in the womb to be a non-person. Our Constitution guarantees every citizen the right to life, liberty, and the pursuit of happiness. Each child in the womb *is* a real person who is guaranteed the right to life.

Each person has the right to choose. We do not, however, have the right to usurp the right to choose for someone else. Terminating the life of an unborn child is usurping the right of that child to choose life. For over fifty years the battle over the slaughter of the innocence has raged on resulting in the death of over 63 million unborn babies. The child that was already conceived and designed by God has the DNA, the blueprint for every part of what that child will be.

Methods used to cause or perform an abortion:

"Contraceptive" drugs and devices – In the first week of life these cause micro-abortions. The morning-after pill prevents implantation of the tiny new human being. The baby is discarded and flushed from the mother's body.

After implantation, there are drugs such as RU 486 and the IUD (intrauterine device) which cause the child to be expelled from the womb.

On April 21, 2023 in Washington, the Supreme Court allowed the most commonly used abortion pill mifepristone to remain widely available. Women can still obtain mifepristone by mail and use it up to ten weeks into a pregnancy. Abortion opponents continue to fight against it.

In the first trimester, there are surgical methods of abortion that literally cut the baby to pieces or the suction method that tears the baby apart which the baby can feel in excruciating pain.

In the second trimester, most commonly in the 1970s and '80s, was the saline or salt poisoning method which takes over an hour to kill the baby who struggles and dies a very slow agonizing death.

In the third trimester, is the partial birth abortion method whereby the baby is partially drawn out like a breech delivery, then a scissors is inserted into the base of the skull, and the brain is sucked out resulting in unbelievable pain for the baby and then death.

There are also other methods used which are just as horrific and painful for the baby as these.

The Abortion Issue

Dangers to the mother:

Some women become unable to bear children ever again. Physical complications including infections and hemorrhage have occurred sometimes resulting in death.

Even more common are the psychological scars that remain with the mother for the rest of her life.

What about rape or incest? The psychological scars from such an occurrence can last a lifetime. If keeping the baby is too emotionally stressing for a woman, she can always give the baby up for adoption. If she chooses abortion, not only will she continually face the memory of the rape or incestuous encounter, but she will always carry the burden of guilt knowing she murdered her own child. Carrying that guilt is far more detrimental to her wellbeing than giving up the baby for adoption.

Victims of abortions:

The baby is the main victim, dying in excruciating pain.

The mother who suffers physical and psychological anguish for a long time many times known only to herself.

Murdered women who refuse to get an abortion. Usually the father wants to hide the adulterous affair from his wife and the rest of the family.

The father who wants the baby to live, but has no say in the matter.

A young teenage girl who was taken advantage of by an older "boyfriend" or a married man who doesn't want his wife to know. She may be taken across state lines so her parents won't know about the abortion.

Victims of rape or incest who suffer and the baby is punished by death because of the wrong doing of a selfish man.

Grandparents and other family members who grieve over the grandchild that will never be.

The abortionist who finally comes to realize the evil that was done and finds himself/herself riddled with guilt, doesn't know how to cope with the guilt, turns to drugs/alcohol to dull the pain, and ends up destroying another life – his/her own.

The taxpayers who do not want their hard-earned money going to pay for abortions that they do not want but end up having it shoved down their throats.

Hospitals, doctors, nurses, pharmacists, and other health professionals who are forced to participate in abortions or forced to close their doors – forcing them to give up the profession for which they are trained.

Future Social Security recipients who will not have enough money coming in because of all those babies who would now be paying into the system but were not allowed to be thus allowing Social Security to become bankrupt.

The abortion industry is very lucrative and the abortionist doesn't care who gets hurt in the process that is until it catches up with him/her. Sooner or later all evil catches up with the perpetrator.

What does the future hold?

"In Roe v. Wade, the Supreme Court decided that the right to privacy implied in the 14th Amendment protected abortion as a fundamental right. However, the government retained the power to regulate or restrict abortion access depending on the stage of pregnancy."[84]

On June 24, 2022, the Supreme Court ruled in Dobbs v. Jackson Women's Health Organization – a case involving a challenge to a Mississippi ban on abortion at 15 weeks of pregnancy. The ruling

---

[84] Brennan Center for Justice

overturned Roe v. Wade ending the Constitutional right to abortion in the United States. The Supreme Court determined that women do not have a Constitutional right to choose to terminate their pregnancies and overturned the long-standing 50-year precedent established in Roe v. Wade. This means that the legal authority to decide on the abortion issue now reverts back to the states where it belongs. Each state has the authority to determine whether abortion will be legal in that state, what kinds of restrictions will be enforced, or whether abortion will be completely banned.

Some states are keeping abortion legal, some are imposing more strict regulations, and some states are working to ban abortion completely. While the battle rages on regarding women's rights, one factor is overlooked – the rights of the baby. Our Constitution does not mention any right to abortion. It does, however, mention the right of every person to life, liberty, and the pursuit of happiness. ***The baby is a real person and is guaranteed the right to life by the Constitution of the United States of America.*** No one should be allowed to take that right away.

Appendix D

The Warning: Illumination Of Conscience And The Miracle

There have been a number of people who have related an experience of being close to death, perhaps it was a near-death experience where their whole life flashed before their eyes. How does this happen and why?

The Blessed Mother Mary told Sister Lucy of Fatima, Portugal, "Wars are a punishment for the sins of mankind." More people of all faiths believe that we are in "the end of times" – not the end of the world, but the end of an age or era of time. The earth is immersed in an era of much grievous sin and the Lord God will soon take steps to remedy this situation. Satan knows that his time is short. That is the reason that there is so much evil manifested in these times, most especially the evil of abortion – the murder of the innocent baby in the womb.

The Blessed Mother has appeared to quite a number of visionaries across the globe many times. Her messages are always centered on *conversion and amendment of life.* When she appeared at Garabandal, Spain on October 18, 1961 to four young girls, ages 11 and 12, she spoke about two events that would happen, the Warning and the Great Miracle.

"To the Eucharist there is given less and less importance. If you ask pardon with a sincere soul, He (God) will pardon you. It is I, your Mother, wish to say that you amend, that you are already in the last warnings and that I love you much and do not want your condemnation. Ask us sincerely and we will give it to you. You should sacrifice more. Think of the Passion of Jesus." Her greatest emphasis was placed on the Eucharist and the priesthood.

The Warning – The Illumination of Consciences

What is the illumination of Consciences? How will it come about?

All light from the sun will be extinguished and a dense darkness will cover the entire earth. A brilliant light will be seen in the sky and will show Jesus Christ on the cross. Everyone on the earth will be able to see it.

On June 12, 1965, Conchita, one of the visionaries, wrote, "The Warning, like the chastisement, is a fearful thing for the good as well as the wicked. It will draw the good closer to God and warn the wicked the end of times is coming." Every person will see their past sins and the consequences of those sins affecting each person including how those sins affect other people. *All* people will experience this illumination of conscience including those who don't believe in God.

This is a tremendous gift of mercy from God allowing each person to ***choose*** to change his/her behavior and avoid the ***eternal*** punishment of hell that is due to their sins. We ***will all*** be held accountable for our deeds – the good and the bad. Each person at the end of his/her life will experience an illumination of conscience – their whole life flashes before their eyes. This is the particular judgment of a person. There is no reason to be fearful. God will affect this **Warning** with justice and love. Many souls will repent of their sins and change their behavior resulting in the salvation of their soul.

Jesus told Jamie Garza, mystic and stigmatist, "...the illumination that will take place will be for a short time. During this time My Father will allow all of humanity to see the state of their souls as My Father sees their souls. This will be a time of great grace when many souls will repent and return to My Father. Those souls that die will die of great shock to see the state of darkness which exists in their souls."[85]

Jesus told Saint Faustina Kowalska, "Let the greatest sinner place their trust in My mercy. They have the right before others to trust in the abyss of My mercy. My daughter, write about My mercy towards tormented souls. Souls that make an appeal to My mercy delight Me. To such souls I grant even more graces than they ask. I cannot punish even the greatest sinner if he make an appeal to My compassion, but on the contrary, I justify him in My unfathomable and inscrutable mercy."[86]

The Blessed Mother said on Pentecost May 22, 1988, that the Warning is the **Second Pentecost**. "This is the day which recalls the descent of the Holy Spirit upon the Apostles...On this day of *Pentecost of the Marian Year, consecrated to me,* I am calling upon you to unite your prayer to that of your heavenly Mother, to obtain *the great gift of the* **Second Pentecost**...The Holy Spirit will come...which will renew all the world...the Church will open itself to live the new era of its greatest holiness...that will attract to itself all the nations of the earth. The Holy Spirit will come, that the Will of the Heavenly Father be accomplished and the created universe once again reflect His great glory...to establish the glorious reign of Christ, and it will be a

---

[85]   Jamie Garza, United States, (1955-), Wife, Mother, Mystic, Stigmatist

[86]   Diary of Saint Maria Faustina Kowalska, #1146

reign of grace, holiness, love of justice and of peace. The Holy Spirit will come, by means of triumph of my Immaculate Heart. We will see ourselves in the *burning fire of divine truth, a judgment in miniature, that will illuminate all consciences."*

The Blessed Mother also said that there will be a **Great Miracle** that will take place within a year after the Warning. It will be seen in the sky, be able to be photographed and televised, but not be able to be touched. There will be a **Permanent Sign** that will be located at the Pines at Garabandal. It can be seen by anyone who goes to Garabandal. However, no one will be able to touch it. It will be an undeniable act of God.

If you are having trouble believing in all of this, check it out for yourself. There are many saints and visionaries as well as ordinary people who have had messages, visions, experiences, all with remarkable similarities. All this cannot be just a coincidence. You can find much information in libraries, on the Internet, in book stores.

Check it out for yourself

Bibiography

"Dr. Alveda King - Sorrow that Dr. Tiller Didn't Live to Repent," Christian Newswire

"Profile: George Tiller," BBC News/America

Alexander, Eban, Proof of Heaven A Neurosurgeon's Journey into Afterlife, Simon & Schuster, NY

Amorth, Gabriele, An Exorcist Tells His Story, Ignatius Press, San Francisco, CA, 1999

Arendzen, J. P., Purgatory and Heaven, Tan Books and Publishers, Rockford, IL, 1972

Bemelmans, Benoit, Jacinta of Fatima, Crusade Magazine, July/August 2017

Bodansky, Yossef, Bin Laden: The Man Who Declared War On America

Brennan Center for Justice

Burpo, Todd, Heaven is for Real, Thomas Nelson, Inc. Nashville, Tennessee

Caine, K W & B P Kaufman, Prayer, Faith and Healing, Rodale Press, Emmaus, PA, 1999

Catechism of the Catholic Church, Libreria Editrice Vaticana, English Translation, 1994

Catholic Encyclopedia, "Heaven"

Catholic Encyclopedia, "St. Mary of Egypt," Vol. 9, Robert Appleton Co., NewYork

Duin, Julia, "Bernard Nathanson's Conversion," www.ewtn.com/library/profile/berconv.txt

Father Speaks To His Children, The, "Pater" Publications, Kansas City, MO, 1999

Garza, Jamie, United States, (1955-), Wife, Mother, Mystic, Stigmatist

Glenn, Msgr. Paul J., A Tour of the Summa

Gonzalez-Balado, Jose Luis, Mother Teresa: Her Life, Her Work, Her Message

Hays, Tom, Larry Neumeister, "Madoff geats maximum," AP, Hazleton Standard-Speaker, 2009

Holy Love Messages, Holy Love Ministries, Maranatha Spring & Shrine, Elyria, OH, 2010

Horvat II, John, ront Alley Abortions, Crusade Magazine, July/August 2011

Kowalska, Sister M. Faustina, Diary of, Divine Mercy in My Soul

Kushner, S., When Bad Thing Happen to Good People, Anchor Books, Random House, NY 1981

Lopez, Kathryn Jean, "The Wrong Release," The Corner, National Review

BIBIOGRAPHY

Lubold; Youssef; Coles; "Iran Fires Missiles at US Forces in Iraq," The Wall Street Journal, 1/7/2020

Maniyangat, Fr. Jose, Life After Death Experience, Website: frmaniyangathealing ministry.com

Meeting-the-Father Ministry, Inc., Eileen George: Beacon of God's Love, Millbury, MA

Murray, J. O'Kane, Little Lives of the Great Saints, Tan Books & Publishers, Rockford, IL, 1977

Nathanson, Bernard, M.D., "Confession of An Ex-Abortionist", www.aboutabortions.com/Confess

Neal, Mary C., To Heaven And Back, Waterback Press, Random House, New York

Newsmax, April 2023, pp. 46-52

Piper, Don, 90 Minutes in Heave, Guideposts, Carmel, New York, 2004

Pope John Paul II, On The Christian Meaning of Human Suffering,Salvifici Doloris, 1984

Puhak, Msgr. N I, St. Mary's Byzantine Catholic Church, Hazleton Standard Speake, 8/14/2010

Reuters

Ritchie, George, Return from Tomorrow, Guidposts Edition

Romero, Jesse, Life Changing Srories of the Eucharist, Lighthouse Catholic Media, 2012

Rosary stopped Ted Bundy,snopes.com

Rosenberg, Joel C., Inside the Revolution, Tyndale House Publishers, C AtreM, IL, 2009

Schmidt, A. M., To Hell and Back, Divine Love and the Cross, Lighthouse Catholic Media, 2012

Schmoger, C E, The Life of Jesus Christ, Visions: A C Emmerich, Tan Publishers, Rockford, IL

Schouppe, Fr. F. X., S.J. Hell, Tan Books & Publishers, Rockford, IL, 1989

Simi & Segreti, St. Francis of Paola

Wikipedia, Amish school shooting

Wikipedia, Karla Faye Tucker

Wikipedia, Martin Luther King, Jr.,

All Biblical references are taken from:

Saint Joseph Holy Bible, Douay Version,

Catholic Book Publishing Co., New York

The New American Bible,

Thomas Nelson Publishers,

Nashville, Camden, New York

Order Information

Did you enjoy this book? Were you uplifted, encouraged, or helped by it? Is there someone you know who could benefit from reading this book? Share your experience.

Check out local libraries, bookstores, Amazon.com, and the Internet.

For a book or ebook – Go to Amazon.com and type in: SHENYO.

Thank you and God bless you.

About the Author

Patricia Klatch Shenyo is an ordinary person like most of us – a wife, mother, grandmother, and by profession a high school Business Education teacher, now retired.

Mrs. Shenyo has a style of writing that is warm, inviting, and at the same time intriguing. She "carries on a conversation" with the reader and allows him/her to feel perfectly comfortable in some not-so-comfortable situations. The reader is very much attracted by the sincerity and compassion exhibited by the author. Her message is so compelling as to urge the reader to share it with family, friends, and anyone who is willing to listen. Her work is very clear and answers many questions about life's many difficult circumstances.

Mrs. Shenyo has authored, in addition to this new book, her book entitled **God?** – First and Second Editions. She also developed a project for her students whereby they could investigate specific careers according to their abilities and interests. The project was highly successful leading to two small books designed to help high school and college students decide on and prepare for a career as well as pursuing suitable employment. They are entitled **Making Wise Career Choices** and **Getting The Job You Desire**. These are available on Amazon.com. Just type in SHENYO.

Made in the USA
Middletown, DE
17 April 2024